LIVE SMART

Praise for *Live Smart*

'I love that in an era of YouTube and a million ideas that often don't work, you have a solid book, full of tried and tested life hacks to help you Live Smart. I could be stranded on an island with this book and you can be assured that I'll be fine!'

—Rukmini Ray Kadam, blogger and founder of the award-winning décor blog *Trumatter*

'Sensible, small hacks in the important areas of life are the must-have skills today in the post-pandemic world. Teja Lele's book is a perfect way to learn these. The book has plenty of painstakingly put-together helpful hacks that can be applied in our daily life. It is a must-read! *Live Smart* can help you lead a quality life with simple hacks that span beauty, well-being, home and food. It is vital reading for today's generation.'

—Kavita Devgan, author

'In India where the DIY culture is weak, even decried, a book on ways to solve common household problems without recourse to a tradesperson cannot but be appropriate. ... Teja's excellent little book is replete with examples of how a lay person could well tackle the myriad problems of daily life. Her list of useful instructions include essential tasks such as changing a blown fuse to recycling kitchen waste. There are tips on health, beauty, quick recipes and much else. In all, this delightful little compendium should be in the home of every Indian.'

—Indranil Banerjie, journalist, woodworker and founder of the popular blog *The Indian DIY & Woodworker*

LIVE SMART

100 HACKS FOR A HEALTHIER AND HAPPIER LIFE

TEJA LELE

HarperCollins *Publishers* India

First published in India by HarperCollins *Publishers* 2022
4th Floor, Tower A, Building No. 10, Phase II, DLF Cyber City,
Gurugram, Haryana – 122002
www.harpercollins.co.in

2 4 6 8 10 9 7 5 3 1

P-ISBN: 978-93-9440-788-6
E-ISBN: 978-93-9440-789-3

Typeset in 11/14 Raleway at
Manipal Technologies Limited, Manipal

Inside Illustrations by Surojit Bhattacharjee

Printed and bound at
Thomson Press (India) Ltd

For Aai and Baba, the wind beneath my wings

CONTENTS

SECTION 2: FOOD AND KITCHEN

SECTION 3: BEAUTY

SECTION 4: HEALTH AND WELL-BEING

SECTION 5: REUSE AND RECYCLE

INTRODUCTION

'Happiness belongs to the self-sufficient.'

—Aristotle

In a past life, I must have been a homesteader. Waking up at the crack of dawn, milking cows, raising chickens, keeping bees, growing vegetables, preserving food, setting up a rain barrel, upcycling textiles, making my own medicines ... My forebears did it all. How could I have not? My inner do-it-yourself (DIY) freak often goes on trips that let me relive the simple, off-the-grid lifestyle that offers the chance to do it all myself.

In my mind's eye, I see myself as *Gone with the Wind*'s Scarlett O'Hara, silhouetted against the setting sun as she worked the fields near Tara, her large family home.

Well, homestead really!

In this life, however, I am much too dependent on other people to ever pass off as a homesteader. A leaking tap means calling the plumber, the onset of summer means reminding the HVAC guy to clean the air-conditioner filters, and a tooth twinge means running to the dentist. Also, the tube light won't switch on — so *where* is the electrician already?

Self-sustainability doesn't come easy in today's world, where almost everything we need is a click or a swipe away. Inexpensive labour has rendered most of us unable to do even the smallest of repairs and chores by ourselves, and the availability of doorstep delivery and online options ensures that we never need to step out of our comfort zone, unless absolutely necessary.

The year 2020 made it NECESSARY.

The COVID-19 pandemic shook the world up – upending nations, businesses, workplaces, and homes. While Indian Prime Minister Narendra Modi made '*aatmanirbhar*' (self-reliant) a part of our lexicon only after he announced Unlock 1.0, India was already waking up to the importance of being self-sufficient during the COVID-19 lockdown.

The pandemic was a great leveller, confining everyone to their homes, without the help we were used to getting. Be it cooking or gardening, beauty treatments or health issues, electrical jobs or plumbing problems — we had to learn to handle everything on our own. If we couldn't, we just had to do without. This was a rude wake-up call to millions of people who were previously used to outsourcing every possible domestic task to helpers and specialists.

The disturbing global event, which claimed millions of lives, adversely affected economies, food supply security, and health and wellness, also led us to think about becoming less complacent. Self-reliance was the only thing that kept us going during those long, locked-in months.

The lockdowns may now be behind us, but our need to be self-sufficient hasn't gone away. The idea of 'self-sufficiency' has for long been used interchangeably with the concept of 'homesteading' – the latter being associated with large acreages of land where people grew their own food, tended to animals and livestock, canned and preserved food and grain, made their own soaps and cleaners, and practised simple living. This lifestyle choice, which was often used by governments in the past to help people put down roots in previously unsettled areas, advocates self-sufficiency.

And coming back to the homestead, my inner Scarlett O'Hara would love to think that I could take the back-to-the-land, survivalism route in the face of challenges and adversity. Yet, my forebears were obviously made of stronger stuff than I am. I possess neither their fortitude and grit, nor their knowledge and expertise. What I do possess, however, is the Indian propensity for 'jugaad' – a flexible approach to problem-solving, using limited resources in an innovative way. The pursuit of a self-sufficient lifestyle may not be easy, but it is possible to hack – or jugaad – your way to self-subsistence. And, in this part of the world, we excel at it.

Hacking is now part of our everyday vocabulary, but the phrase 'life hack' is said to have been coined at a technology conference in 2004. Back then, it meant an inelegant but efficient solution to a computing problem. Over time, the term has quickly become a part of our life, and translates into a tip, trick, shortcut, or method that increases productivity and efficiency. A life hack is meant to free up time by making tasks easier, faster and better to help you live smarter. Be it the internet, magazines, newspapers, or conversations – hacks abound.

Over the last few years, my inclination to DIY has helped me learn new ways of doing important things, tasks that, in the pre-pandemic era, I would have happily handed off to someone else. Along the way, I have come to realize that creating, doing, making, and repairing things not only makes me less dependent on others – no more 'Bhaiyya, sink fix *karne kab aaoge*? (Bhaiyya, when will you come to fix the sink?)' – but also offers a multitude of benefits. It has helped me unlearn a few dogmas, learn new skills, cultivate a sense of accomplishment and pride, save money, and help the environment.

Most importantly, it helps me FOCUS.

At any given point in time, on any day of the week, my laptop has eight to ten tabs open on the browser. The same goes for my mind, where I toggle between the many open tabs – home, work, kitchen, relationships, to-dos, must-dos, and many more – through the day. Having a task at hand, that I must do well, lets me apply my mind solely on one thing and improves my concentration.

I find it extremely therapeutic and restorative, as it mentally transports me into *flow*, a state in which I feel utmost involvement, greater enjoyment, and heightened energy.

WHAT IS FLOW?

In his 1990 book, *Flow: The Psychology of Optimal Experience*, positive psychologist Mihály Csíkszentmihályi writes that flow is a state of complete immersion in an activity. He describes it as 'a state in which people are so involved in an activity that nothing else seems to matter; the experience is so enjoyable that people will continue to do it even at great cost, for the sheer sake of doing it'.

He believes it offers a number of benefits, including a sense of enjoyment and fulfilment, more motivation, amplified engagement, skill development, improved performance and creativity, and – most important of all – increased happiness.

Of course, not everything gives me flow, for not all tasks and odd jobs are created equal. But if getting into the flow of things can help shift happiness levels, isn't it worth doing my own work, chores, repair, maintenance, and upkeep around the home(stead)?

Around the home, this translates into increasing self-sufficiency skills to a level where you can do most things on your own. It may appear daunting, but living smarter is a skill that can be learnt and honed. Apart from shaking out the cobwebs in your mind, it can lead to a better standard of living and a healthier, more rewarding lifestyle. Modern life may have numerous benefits, but it is accompanied by many problems that we are often unaware of – a shrinking attention span, a desire for immediate gratification, intolerance for hard work, and an overall sense of entitlement. And with outsourcing becoming the in thing, the problem has became increasingly pronounced.

But now, with growing awareness, and the desire to do our bit and make a difference, it makes sense to leave behind a few newfangled notions and return to the old ways of doing things. There was a reason our forebears chose to do things a particular way. Adopting their habits and practices could take us back to a natural way of living – much needed in our often-simulated, almost-synthetic lifestyle.

After all, happy hands = happy hearts!

THE BASIC SURVIVAL SKILLS QUIZ

How would you fare if you had to do things that are integral to everyday life, but haven't fallen in your purview yet? Take this quiz and find out.

- ☐ Can you change a flat tyre?
- ☐ Do you know how to jump-start a car?
- ☐ Can you get roaches, lizards, and other bugs out of your room?
- ☐ Can you fix a leaky faucet?
- ☐ Do you know what to do when the kitchen sink gets clogged?
- ☐ Do you know CPR?
- ☐ Do you know how to treat a bee sting?
- ☐ Do you know how to deal with a burn?
- ☐ Do you know how to stem a nosebleed?
- ☐ Can you paint a wall?
- ☐ Do you know how to hang a picture?
- ☐ Can you whip up a meal when the pantry's running dry?
- ☐ Can you make a full meal without a recipe?
- ☐ Can you make a main course dish with kitchen scraps?
- ☐ Can you make your own lotion/cream?
- ☐ Can you rustle up a deodorant in the kitchen?
- ☐ Can you make your own mouthwash?
- ☐ Can you grow your own microgreens?
- ☐ Can you compost your kitchen waste?
- ☐ Do you know how to upcycle fruit and veggie peels?
- ☐ Do you know how to replace a light fixture?
- ☐ Can you purify water if the purifier stops working?
- ☐ Will you be able to take care of a sudden stomach ache?
- ☐ Do you know an easy way to take care of a fever?
- ☐ Can you resolve the 'mosquitoes in the balcony' issue?

Give yourself 4 points for every yes.

90-100: You're a homesteader, a survivalist.

80-50: You won't be lonesome on your ownsome as you have so much to do.

70-79: You could survive on your own for a while, but could do with more learning.

50 and below: You need to skill up – and NOW!

Let's get started.

HOW TO USE THIS BOOK

Live Smart: 100 Hacks for a Healthier and Happier Life is divided into five sections, each focusing on a different aspect of life – Home, Food and Kitchen, Beauty, Health and Well-being, and Reuse and Recycle. Together, they encompass almost all facets of our daily life, aspects that we must stay on top of, to achieve that ever-elusive peace of mind.

This book includes some important and not-to-be-missed tips for anyone keen on taking the first steps to becoming self-sufficient, as well as those who have the ultimate and lofty goal of becoming a true survivalist.

Knowing how to unplug a clogged sink, tackling a toothache or earache if a doctor isn't available, reviving an old piece of furniture, or growing veggies from scraps may not seem all that arduous, but they aren't exactly easy when push comes to shove. *Live Smart* aims to give you simpler, easier, and uncomplicated ways to do the many tasks that adulting demands of everyone. It offers a comprehensive, albeit not exhaustive, list of hacks needed to simplify your life. Most of these hacks are very doable, and require only basic tools and materials that are easily available at home. There's no need to rush to the shops – something that most of us begin our DIY projects with, defeating the very purpose and essence of DIY. We want to make do with what we have, and looking around the home with a practised eye can help do that.

The book may be divided into specific chapters, but that doesn't mean that you need to follow the laid-out path. Go where your fancy takes you – start from page 1, dive into page 73, or begin reading backwards in your pursuit of a self-sufficient lifestyle.

WHY YOU NEED THIS BOOK

Our hectic modern way of living has most of us yearning for a simpler, more meaningful life, but not many of us really know what that entails or how to take the first step towards achieving it. Does it mean harking back to the past and growing your own vegetables, does it mean cutting your spends to zero, or does it mean living below your means? It can be a tad confusing, especially when some words are often (incorrectly) used interchangeably when it comes to the makeup of a simpler life.

Minimalism: The excesses of modern life have given way to the need to practise minimalism, a way of life characterized by severe spareness and simplicity. At home, this translates into constant purges and edits, so that we end up owning only those things that we truly need.

Old-fashioned living: The way thrifty Grandma lived 'back in the day' definitely had less stress and clutter, and more self-sufficiency. In today's time, this translates into living the way she did: making things, sewing clothes, going for walks, sleeping early, and being content with what we have.

Frugal living: A way of life that helps us be very intentional with our spending, so that we live below our means and save as much money as possible. It doesn't mean denying ourselves; it simply advocates spending on those things that matter and weeding out those that don't.

Slow living: Born out of the slow food movement, which underlines the importance of local and traditional food over fast food, slow living advocates a lifestyle that's about consuming less and taking a slower, more measured approach to everyday life.

So, what is a self-sufficient lifestyle? Is it one of these, or a set of values that's completely different?

Honestly, it's all this and more.

Being self-sufficient means different things to different people. To me, it may mean creating my homestead (yes, that again!) in the middle of an urban jungle (after all, tomatoes and coriander can be grown in pots on the terrace); to my friend, it may translate into embracing frugality and trying to ditch debt. To her friend, it may mean downsizing and editing their oversized lifestyle; to you, it may denote becoming the house handyman.

Whatever self-sufficiency means to each of us, the ultimate aim is the same: learning to provide for our own needs.

In a world that's active 24X7 and where almost everything is available round the clock, this book should be on your to-read list if you want to:

✓ Prioritize what's important to you

- ✓ Master new skills
- ✓ Learn to be self-reliant
- ✓ Be more resilient
- ✓ Enhance your self-esteem
- ✓ Gain a sense of achievement
- ✓ Save money
- ✓ Become a conscious consumer
- ✓ Make realistic and sustainable trade-offs
- ✓ Focus on your passions
- ✓ Make yourself happier

Living smart and adopting a self-sufficient lifestyle may not be the panacea for all the maladies of modern life, but it's a small step towards acquiring a spirit of independence and wresting back control over our lives.

Isn't that reason enough to leave the 'coulda, woulda, shoulda' out of the equation and ingrain a sense of sureness, confidence, and conviction to hit (almost) every curveball life hurls at us?

Let's get started.

SECTION 1

HOME

'There is nothing like staying at home for real comfort.'
—Jane Austen

Close your eyes and think of a happy place. Chances are your mind will take you to an inviting beach or a gorgeous mountainside. *Ah, nothing beats a summer vacation, does it?* I am no different; vacations make me really happy. Yet, there's only one place that makes me joyful: home.

Home isn't just a place where we happen to reside in; it's a repository of memories, remembrances, love, laughter, affection, and so much more. Beams and bricks make up structures, but it's the people that populate a particular house and their relationships that transform it into home.

Clichéd? Yes. But true? Also yes!

The 2020 pandemic gave every home many new avatars. My home, too, was no longer just a place we lived in: it was an office, a school, a gym, a yoga studio, a bakery, a play centre, a movie theatre and more, all rolled into one. Much like the Room of Requirement in Harry Potter's beloved Hogwarts, it was a montage of shifting spaces that kept pace with our changing needs.

While our home provides us with the centring we need, it also demands our time and effort to maintain sanctuary status. Home sweet home, yes, but not if you fail to keep up with the upkeep. For no home is ever 'complete'. Every time I think mine is, something comes back to haunt me.

Think about it. Doesn't the home have a way of showing you your place if you don't give it the TLC it needs? Slowly but surely, things fall apart. The sink clogs up; the washing machine goes *phut*; piles of washed clothes take over the bedroom; the couch becomes a playground for stains of all kinds; and the flat tyre cocks a snook at you, keeping you confined at home!

Whoever thought home management was doing a few chores in the morning and chipping in with a few during the week clearly had no idea what they were talking about. A home is always a work in progress, one that you keep adding to, subtracting from, making changes to, and planning transformations for. It's a *continual*, unending process.

I find myself doing it everyday – cleaning, sorting, organizing, doing the laundry, menu planning, grocery shopping, cooking, home improvements – and then I wake up the next morning and do it all over again!

Shirking doesn't work, for there's no getting away from the fact that home management is a *must* that needs to be actioned each and every day. And that it's important for everyone to be able to do basic tasks, repairs, and improvements around the home – without calling in specialists to help. Apart from an increased sense of satisfaction and self-worth, this ability taps into our primal need to take care of our homes – which seems hardwired into the human DNA. Looking after the many parts that make up the whole ensures that the household runs in a smooth and systematic way, and gives you a place that you want to come home to. And while it may sound overwhelming at first, acing home how-tos isn't tough; all you need to do is get started.

BASIC HOME TOOL KIT

You can't ensure the upkeep of your haven without the right tools. Keep them handy so you can get down to business as soon as needed.

Tools

- Hammer
- Pliers
- Screwdrivers, of different sizes
- Cordless drill, and drill bit set
- Adjustable wrench
- Scissors
- Utility knife
- Wire stripper
- Staple gun
- Clamps

Hardware

- Nails and screws
- Screw eyes
- Nuts and bolts
- Plastic anchors
- Picture hooks and wires
- Cup hooks
- Command hooks

Others

- 12-inch metal ruler
- Tape measure
- Level
- Flashlight
- Sandpaper
- Carpenter's glue
- Instant adhesive
- White glue
- Tape
- Adhesive remover

ELECTRICAL

1.

FIX A BLOWN FUSE

A blown fuse is common, but do you know why it happens? An imbalance between the maximum amount of amperes that the fuse is rated for and the power load in your house can lead to this. This happens when too many electric appliances run at the same time, or the electric load surpasses the maximum load. When a fuse blows, it actually prevents your home and appliances from extensive damage. Replacing a fuse is a relatively easy task that you can DIY.

What you need **Time < 45 minutes**

✓ Wire cutter
✓ Pliers
✓ Screwdriver
✓ Fuse wire

How

- Unplug appliances that pull heavy load, such as the refrigerator and air-conditioners. Don't forget to unplug new appliances, too.
- Locate the electrical panel. This is usually located high up on the wall, near the entrance to your home. Ensure your hands

are dry, and wear rubber-soled footwear to avoid electrocution. Never use a metal trunk as an elevation to reach the panel; use a wooden piece of furniture.

- The panel may contain circuit breakers or fuses. In case you have circuit breakers, look for one that has moved to the 'off' position, or is in between the 'on' and 'off' position. This is the breaker causing the problem. Move it to the 'on' position if it is 'off'. If it is stuck between the 'on' and 'off' positions, move it to 'off' and then switch it 'on'.
- If the panel has a fuse box, check each fuse to see if the wire inside has melted or if the glass window on top of it is discoloured. This may be time-consuming, but needs to be done.
- Once you have found the blown fuse, turn the 'Main' switch off to cut the flow of electricity. Unscrew the broken fuse and bring out the fuse wire with the correct amp rating.
- Loosen the terminal screws, and remove the old and broken wire. Cut the new fuse wire: it should be long enough to wrap around both terminal screws and cross the fuse carrier. Wind the wire around one terminal screw clockwise and tighten this screw into place.
- Look at one of the working fuses to see how to wire up the blown fuse. You will need to either thread the wire through the fuse holder or pass it through the bridge. Wind the wire around the other terminal screw, clockwise, and leave it a little slack.
- Tighten the final terminal screw and replace the fuse carrier. Close and turn the main switch on again. And let there be light!

2.

REPLACE A LIGHT SWITCH

There can be many reasons to replace a light switch: it loosens up, there's a delay between flipping the switch and the light turning on, it begins to heat up, or it emits noises. Nothing warrants waiting for an electrician. All you need to do is choose a new switch of the same model and get started.

What you need **Time** < 45 minutes

✓ Needle-nose pliers
✓ Screwdriver
✓ Light switch
✓ Switch plate

How

- Turn off the power to the light switch at the main circuit-breaker box. Use a screwdriver to remove the old wall plate. Disconnect the old switch by removing all the screws. Pull out the switch and the attached wires. Be careful not to damage any wires.
- Most switches have three types of wires: black wires (attached to black/brass screws), copper/green ground wires (attached to green/copper/grounding screws), and neutral white wires.

When you turn on a light switch, the power goes to the light fixture through the hot (black) wire and then through the neutral (white) wire to the ground. The grounding wires are a backup in case of an electrical fault.

- Use a screwdriver to release the wires if attached with push-in connectors. Make sure the new wall plate fits and the switch is oriented right. Then, attach the new wires to the new switch in the same order as you removed them. Screw the new switch back on and check if everything is in good working order.

3.

SWAP A LIGHT FIXTURE

Changing a light fixture can do more than you think. This high-impact move can create a brand new look in any space, depending on the kind of light you use – warm white, yellow, or bright. Make light work of this project, without waiting for the electrician.

What you need **Time** > 1 hour

- ✓ Wire cutter
- ✓ Screwdriver
- ✓ Circuit tester/Voltage detector
- ✓ Light fixture
- ✓ Wire connectors

How

- Cut the power off at the light switch and at the circuit breaker. Light fixtures are attached to the electrical outlet with bolts or screws. Loosen the hardware and remove the cover of the old fixture until it comes away from the wall or ceiling. At this point, it will still be connected to the electrical wires.

- Most fixtures have three wires: hot (black), neutral (white), and ground (copper). Use a current detector to make sure there's no electrical current running. After that, slowly disconnect all the wires. Make sure you're holding the fixture while you do this.
- Many light fixtures come with a universal bracket that can attach to many kinds of electrical boxes. Secure the bracket to the electrical box with a screwdriver. Follow the manufacturer's instructions to connect the wires. Black wires typically connect with black wires, while white joins white. The grounding wire – made of copper and often green – connects to a grounding screw on the grounding bar. Entwine the bare section of each wire with the bare section of the corresponding existing wire, and screw on the wire connectors.
- Fold the wires into the electrical box and use the included hardware to attach the fixture's base or canopy. Here, you may need a helping hand – especially while replacing a fixture on a high ceiling.
- Finally, install the recommended bulbs. Turn on the circuit's electrical panel and then hit the light switch.

4.

REPLACE AN EXTENSION CORD PLUG

Extension cords are pressed into service around the home to provide your appliances with the power they need. Over time, the stretching and straightening can kill the plug, but replacing it is easy if you know how to.

What you need **Time** < 30 minutes

✓ Screwdriver
✓ Wire cutter
✓ Utility knife
✓ Wire stripper
✓ Replacement plug

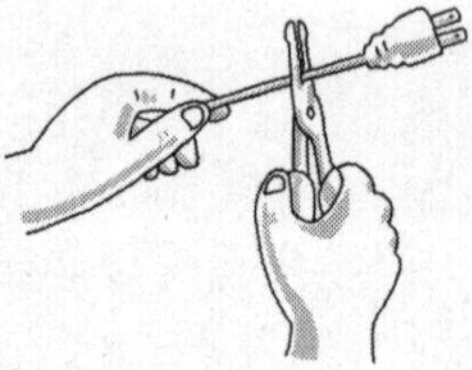

How

- Unplug the cord from any power source, and cut off the old plug using wire cutters. Slide the new plug – with the same amperage and voltage ratings as the cord – over the cut end. Set it aside.

- Use the knife to cut through the outer jacket of the cord. Don't cut all the way through, as this may damage the insulation and set you up for a shock.

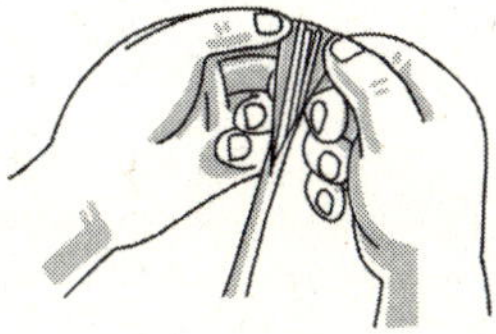

- Split the jacket with your fingernails. Cut off the loose jacket. Use the wire strippers to remove about three-quarters of an inch of the outer insulation from the end of each conducting wire inside the cord.

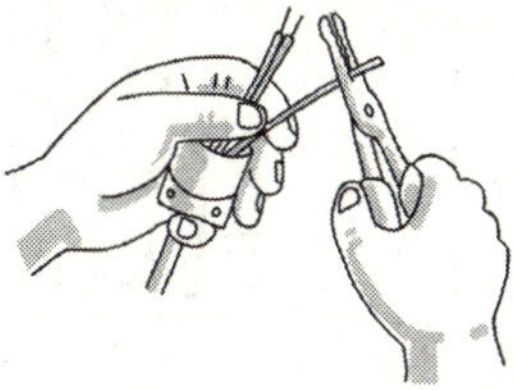

- Use the screwdriver to loosen the terminal screws on the plug. Wrap the bare end of the black (hot) wire clockwise around the brass terminal, and tighten the screw. Wrapping it clockwise ensures that the wire loop tightens around the screw as the screw is tightened.

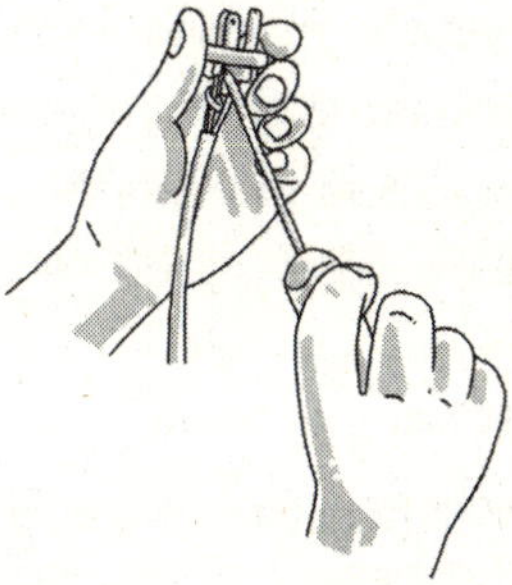

- Connect the white (neutral) wire to the silver terminal and the green (ground) wire to the ground screw. The ground screw may be marked with green and is always connected to the U-shaped ground prong. Double-check the connections for tightness by tugging gently on each wire.
- Join the two parts with the provided screws and tighten the cord clamp on the body. Plug into a socket to check if it is working.

5.

REDUCE YOUR ELECTRICITY BILL

Keeping the lights on isn't cheap – not to forget the air conditioning, washing machine, refrigerator, TVs, and laptops. A typical home ends up spending a lot on power – as much as Rs 2,000 per month in winters and more than Rs 10,000 per month in summers. Cutting these costs is good – for the environment *and* for your wallet!

What you need

✓ A desire to save energy – and save money

How

- **Check your lighting:** Switch to low-consumption LED lighting or CFLs (which are five times more efficient than normal bulbs) and make sure you dust your lights and bulbs regularly. Dirty fixtures absorb more and reflect less light. A reading lamp ensures you use less energy.
- **Monitor the AC:** The air-conditioner adds significantly to your electricity bill for at least six months in a year. Set the temperature

at 26°C to maintain optimal cooling, and shade windows and walls to slash bills by at least 40 per cent. Clean the AC filter every month (See Hack 10) to ensure it functions optimally.

- **Inspect the refrigerator:** Keep refrigerators away from all sources of heat, including sunlight, gas stoves, and ovens. Place food inside only after it has cooled down to ensure the fridge doesn't consume more energy. Old refrigerators tend to suck a lot of electricity, so replace with a newer, more efficient model.
- **Cook in bulk:** A modern oven uses, on average, around 2,400 watts on medium to high heat per hour, so make the most of it. Avoid running the oven to cook a small meal. Use every shelf – for bakes, roasts, and more – to get your weekly meal prep sorted while cutting your bill. Freeze the extras.
- **Wash clothes right:** Using cold water can cut your per-load energy usage by at least half. Run a full load to save water, electricity, and detergent (See Hack 19). Using a dryer is a criminal waste of energy in a country that gets so much sunshine. Let your towels, sheets, and apparel air dry on the clothesline to ensure natural disinfection – and save energy.
- **Unplug appliances when not in use:** If you don't really use the mixer all the time, why keep it plugged in? The same goes for the electric kettle, laptop plug, phone charger, and so many other appliances. Unplug and switch off.
- **Install solar panels:** Some parts of India see more than 300 days of sunshine every year, so it makes sense to harness solar energy. Solar panels can be installed on your rooftop and terrace to generate clean energy and shave off your bill considerably. The per kW cost for installing a solar panel is about Rs 50,000; this may seem high, but you'll recover it in a couple of years.

6.

FIX A LEAKY TAP

In addition to wasting water, a leaky faucet can be a source of major irritation. That non-stop drip-drip and your inability to do anything about it means a long wait for the plumber, who fixes it in a jiffy.

What you need **Time < 1 hour**

✓ Screwdriver
✓ Wrench
✓ Washer/O-ring

How

- Turn off the water supply in the bathroom/kitchen. In bathrooms, it tends to be located high up on a dry wall. Find the screw for the tap to locate the cause of the leak. This is easy to find: if you have hot/cold indicators, it is located under them. Unscrew by hand or use a slot-headed screwdriver.
- Remove all decorative parts of the handle knobs with a flat-head screwdriver. The knob will have a screw that mounts the handle on the stem. Unscrew, and gently remove the handle.

Adding a few drops of oil will help loosen screws easily. Lay out all the components in the order in which they were dismantled to make reassembling easier.

- Loosen the packing nut using the wrench; this will let you see the stem. Remove that gently, either by pulling or twisting it off. More likely than not, the problem will be with either the ceramic disc or the washer – a black, circular rubber band. Check the removed parts for damage.
- The O-ring and washer replacements need to be of the right size, so take them to the hardware store and get a packet, if needed. Replace and then reassemble the tap (order: washer/O-ring, stem, packing nut, screw, and handle). Turn the knob to test the tap and check if you've plugged the leak.

7.

REPLACE A SHOWERHEAD

Scanty drips landing on your head and shoulders are not what you want when you step into the bathroom for a cold shower on a hot day, or vice versa. Perhaps it's time to replace the showerhead and also make a small change – get one that uses lesser water.

What you need **Time < 45 minutes**

✓ Showerheads

✓ Pliers

✓ Wrench

How

- Turn the old shower head counter-clockwise to remove it. If you can't unscrew it by hand, grip the shower arm with a pair of pliers, and use a wrench to loosen and unscrew it.
- Screw the new replacement showerhead in a clockwise direction on to the shower arm and tighten. Turn on the water and check for leaks. In case there are some, wrap with thread seal tape and carefully tighten with an adjustable wrench until there are no leaks.

- Position the hand-held shower mount on to the shower arm and screw on by hand. Connect the flexible shower hose to the mount and shower, and tighten the screws. Connect the showerhead to the mount and turn on the water. Check for leaks and, if any, apply thread seal tape.

SMART TIPS

- Change your showerhead *now*. Modern showerheads are much more water efficient than their earlier counterparts – by about 40 per cent.
- Cut your shower time to half. Every minute of shower time that you reduce saves almost 600 litres of water that would otherwise have been wasted each month.
- Sud up and shave before turning on the shower. Shaving your legs in the shower adds about 4 minutes to your bathing routine.
- Clean the showerhead of rust and limescale build-up by wiping it down with a half-and-half solution of vinegar and water.
- If the pores are completely clogged, unscrew the showerhead and let it sit in the solution in a plastic bag for 2 to 8 hours.

8.

UNPLUG A CLOGGED TOILET

There's no need to seek divine intervention when the toilet clogs up. It may not be for the faint-hearted, but it can be done.

What you need **Time > 1 hour**

✓ Plunger
✓ Baking soda
✓ Vinegar/dish soap
✓ Plumbing snake
✓ Wet-dry vacuum

How

- **Use the plunger:** Push the plunger down gently into the toilet bowl until you achieve a good seal, taking care not to splash dirty water on yourself. Pump the plunger up and down forcefully yet gently, maintaining the seal. Pull the plunger up to break the air seal and let the water drain. If the clog stays, repeat the process.

- **Try baking soda:** Add a cup of baking soda to the toilet and let it sit for 2 minutes. Tip in two cups of vinegar slowly, and let the mix bubble. Ensure that the mixture doesn't overflow. Let sit for 10 minutes and flush to see if the clog has cleared. If you're out of vinegar, a large splash of dish soap followed by a litre of hot water will also work.
- **Snake the toilet:** The plumbing snake can help clear persistent clogs and blocks. Put the auger in the toilet bowl and slowly turn it clockwise. Wind the snake back when you feel resistance. Flush the toilet. If the blockage persists, put the snake back in and repeat.

- **Vacuum things up:** This can be done only with a wet-dry vacuum. Begin by vacuuming out all the water from the toilet bowl. Arrange a few old towels or rags in the toilet bowl to create a seal (these will need to be discarded). Stick the vacuum hose a few inches into the toilet drain. Turn on the vacuum and start sucking out the clog.

9.

FIX A SMELLY WASHING MACHINE

The washing machine is meant to churn out clean-smelling laundry day after day, but, over time, soap scum, dirt, body oil, and hair can get trapped inside the washer's seals, gaskets, and dispensers. This makes the machine a breeding ground for mould, mildew, and bacteria. Eliminate the *eww* factor by cleaning your washing machine regularly.

What you need **Time > 1 hour**

✓ Baking soda
✓ Vinegar
✓ Soap

How

- Remove the soap, bleach, and softener dispensers, and scrub thoroughly. An old toothbrush can help clean out cracks and crevices, and remove build-up inside the pipes. In a front-load model, wipe around the rubber seal with a wet cloth, and use wet cotton to remove the gunk around the gasket.

- Sanitize the drum by running a 30-minute cycle with baking soda. Use the highest possible temperature setting to kill all mildew and bacteria.
- The acidic quality of white vinegar removes hard water buildup and all leftover bacteria. Set the machine on the hottest water setting, and add vinegar (4 cups in top-load machine and 2 cups in a front-load model). The 30-minute cycle should get rid of the nastiest of odours. Remove all lint accumulated in the machine's drain trap filter once a week.

SMART TIPS

- Front loaders tend to use a lot less water than top-loader washing machines. They can be more expensive, but think of them as an investment in the environment.
- Never overload the machine, since the clothes need to spin to get clean! But don't underload it either, to avoid wasting energy and water.
- Less is more when it comes to using detergent. Using half the recommended quantity often works well.
- Leave the door of the machine open for about half an hour after every cycle to get rid of moisture, and prevent mould and bacteria buildup.
- Use cold water for delicate fabrics. Warm water is ideal for moderately soiled clothes. Reserve hot water for bedding, towels, and really dirty clothes.

10.

CLEAN THE AC FILTER

Who doesn't love the air-conditioned life in the hot, dusty summer? But it's vital to regularly clean this unit that removes dust and pumps cool air into your rooms. Dirty air filters can make your air conditioner less effective and inflate your electricity bills.

What you need **Time < 2 hours**

✓ Screwdriver
✓ Vacuum cleaner
✓ Vinegar

How

- Use a screwdriver to open the unit and remove the filter. The mesh grid is usually located in the return air duct or blower compartment.
- The plastic mesh filter typically traps dust, dirt, and grime. Wash the filter with running water, and let it dry fully in a well-ventilated space. If very dirty, soak in a large tub for one hour.
- For deeper cleaning, fill a tub with one-part water and one-part white vinegar. Let the filter soak in the solution for one hour.
- Make sure the air filter is completely dry before replacing, to avoid mould.

11.

WALLPAPER LIKE A PRO

If you're looking for an easy fix for a stained wall or just want a new look for a corner, wallpapers can help you do that in a jiffy. They can be an easy fix when you are looking for style at a low cost for any room. In today's time, sticking it on is simple as well: the paste and brush are no longer needed!

What you need

- ✓ Wallpaper
- ✓ Knife
- ✓ Cutter
- ✓ Metal ruler
- ✓ Level
- ✓ Plastic smoother
- ✓ Pencil

Time > 3 hours

How

- Measure the wall's height and depth/length to determine how many rolls of wallpaper you will need. Use a tape measure or one of the many online wallpaper calculators to simplify this.
- Remove all sockets and electrical covers. Wipe down the walls with a damp sponge and a gentle cleanser to remove dust and dirt. Let them dry. Measure the width of the wallpaper. Begin from the left side, and use a tape measure to mark the wall lightly

on the right with a pencil. Put your level on this mark and draw a straight, level, vertical line. This is the guide for your first strip.

- Measure and cut strips of wallpaper to fit the height of the wall. Peel off about 10-12 inches of the backing, line up the top of the paper at the ceiling, and slowly peel and stick the paper down the wall. A plastic smoother can help get rid of air bubbles. Repeat all along the wall. To apply paper along windows, line the wallpaper up along the top and sides of the window. Cut along the edge, peel off the backing, and stick.
- If it's your first time, look for patterns that minimize the tricky matching aspect. A random pattern match – such as a texture – may be a better idea than a design that needs to be aligned both horizontally and vertically with the wallpaper on either side.

SMART TIPS

- If a wallpaper seam appears to be coming apart, use a damp rag to open up the gap. Squeeze white glue into the gap and stick.
- Clean washable wallpaper with a natural sponge dampened with a solution of warm water and liquid dishwashing detergent. Absorb all excess moisture with a cleaning cloth.
- Use baby wipes to clean up ink from washable markers; to get rid of permanent marker stains, dab with rubbing (isopropyl) alcohol.
- Crayon marks on the wallpaper? Scrape away the wax with a blunt knife, and use a paper towel and a warm iron to remove the more stubborn marks.

12.

REVAMP A DAMAGED WALL

Another way to deal with a damaged or stained wall is by getting out the paint bucket and brushes. Dark or light, using paint as an accent can create impact. Rule of thumb: one gallon (3.75 litres) of paint covers about 375–400 square feet of wall area. You're likely to need more paint when going from dark to light.

What you need

- ✓ Paint
- ✓ Paint tray
- ✓ Paint brushes
- ✓ Paint roller
- ✓ Paint roller extension pole
- ✓ Rags and cloths
- ✓ Sandpaper
- ✓ Painter's tape
- ✓ Putty knife

Time > **10 hours**

How

- Use painter's tape on the room's corners, and door and window casings – anywhere you don't want the paint to get. Remove the light switch covers and apply painter's tape to protect them from paint drips. Push all the furniture away from the wall you want to paint and cover with an old sheet/plastic cover.

- Use a damp cloth to wipe down the wall you want to paint, and let it dry. Make sure the wall is smooth and free of holes. Any cracks, holes, or other damage can be filled in with a wall putty paste. Level off with fine-grit sandpaper after it dries. You will need to apply a coat of primer when going from very dark to very light.
- Use a wooden stick to stir the paint, and keep stirring throughout the process. Tip some paint into the tray, dip your roller, and work from the top down – all the way to the bottom. If going from dark to light, you will ideally need three coats – the primer, plus two coats of the new paint colour – but two coats of the paint will also do. Remove the painter's tape. Let dry completely before putting furniture or wall frames back.

SMART TIPS

- Dull paint finishes, such as flat, satin, and eggshell, are less durable when it comes to cleaning. Wipe clean with a wrung-out sponge dipped in an extremely mild dishwashing water solution to get rid of stains.
- Make a paste of a couple of tablespoons of baking soda with warm water and dab the wall stain. Wipe away any residue with a clean, damp cloth. This hack works for most stains.
- For stains on oil-based painted walls/doors, try this simple fix: mix one teaspoon of liquid dish detergent,

a cup of warm water, and 5-6 drops of vinegar. Dab the solution on the stain and blot after 10 minutes.

- To get crayon marks off your walls, fold an old, clean cloth and place over the mark. Run an iron (heated at medium setting) over the cloth. The heat will melt the crayon and transfer the stain on to the cloth. You can also soften the crayon by running a hair dryer over the mark and blot it away with a tissue.

HOW TO DEAL WITH SEEPAGE

Seelan, or seepage, is a common problem, especially during the monsoon. If you can see a crack letting in water, seal it with epoxy or waterproof white cement. Paint after it dries. If the damage is more extensive, you will need to call in the experts to remove the loose plaster and replaster using cement blended with waterproofing compounds. For a quick fix – especially in bathrooms – to remove mould, use a solution of diluted bleach. Read the instructions and do not use on surfaces such as wood or marble. To remove seepage-related mildew from the closets, clean thoroughly with a 50-50 solution of water and vinegar. Wipe down, let air dry, and rub off with water.

13.

REDO OLD FURNITURE

An old wooden chair or table – even if it's laminated – can get a new lease on life after meeting paint. A DIY project that almost anyone can do, painting old wooden furniture can help you upcycle seemingly throwaway items into statement pieces.

What you need

Time < 6 hours

✓ Oil-based primer
✓ Paint
✓ Paint brushes
✓ Foam brushers
✓ Sandpaper

How

Laminated Furniture

- To work with laminated furniture, sand the surfaces in a circular motion using a 150-grit piece of sandpaper. Continue till the entire surface takes on a scuffed appearance. Wipe off the dust and sand again if you feel any large particles/bumps. Apply a coat of oil-based primer with a foam brush. This helps prepare the surface so that the paint can adhere to it.

- Apply two coats of primer, letting it dry in between. Sand using a 320-grit (or higher) sandpaper to smooth out all marks (they will show up after painting, so be very careful). Clean and wipe down.
- Paint the surface in a colour and paint of your choice – acrylic, milk, chalk, or oil. You may need two to three coats of paint for a good finish. Let it dry completely between coats and let stand at least for 12 hours before using.

Wooden Furniture

- To upcycle old wooden furniture, scrape off all the loose paint, remove grime, and sand the surfaces. Apply an oil-based primer to prepare the piece.
- Take a small amount of paint – on the brush or roller – and begin painting. Make sure you move in the same direction all through. Be thorough with the first coat as it provides the base. Let dry for 2-3 hours.
- Use the second coat to ensure an even, glossy coat across the entire length of wood.

SMART TIPS

- Remove dents in wood surfaces with just a damp cloth and iron. Put the cloth on the dent so the wood absorbs the water. Set the iron on its highest setting, place on the damp cloth, and move the iron around. Continue till the cloth is dry.
- Scratches in wooden furniture or floors can be hidden with just a walnut. Rub the nut back and forth across the scratch for 10-15 seconds, and buff the area with a soft microfibre cloth. Out of walnuts? Try an almond.
- Use paraffin wax, which is commonly used for making candles, to smooth out a sticky wooden drawer. All you need to do rub the block of wax along the wooden drawer slides and any other points of friction, and check! Out of wax? Run a candle or wax crayon on the sliders.
- A wobbly table can be so irritating, especially when you are trying to work. Bring out those coins that you no longer use to fix this problem. Dab a coin with some hot glue and slide under the problem area to level out the furniture piece. Or else, slice a piece off a wine cork and glue it in place.
- Stick felt pads to the bottom of chair legs and other movable furniture to prevent them from ruining your floor.

14.

DEAL WITH A DAMAGED FLOOR

Sometimes, a few chipped tiles can really hit the appearance of your space. It may not be the easiest way to transform a room, but changing the flooring can give it a completely new and fresh look – especially if your floor is broken in places or stained heavily. The quickest way is with vinyl tile, which comes in varied thicknesses, colours, and patterns. All you need to do is peel and stick.

What you need

Time > 8 hours

✓ Vinyl floor tiles
✓ Hammer
✓ Utility knife
✓ Tape measure
✓ Floor roller

How

- Determine the area of the room/space where you want to lay vinyl flooring. Divide the square footage to be covered by the square footage contained in a carton of tiles to find out how many boxes you need. Ensure you get 10 per cent extra to make up for waste and future replacements.

- Your new vinyl tiles won't look good if the underlying floor isn't smooth, and free from debris and oil before installation. Clean and mop to avoid any uneven layers, bumps, blemishes, or hollows. Go for the thinnest tile that fits in and lets you open the door (or else you'll need to plane the wood).
- Plan your floor pattern, beginning from the centre (draw chalk lines to find the exact centre). Remove the backing and secure the tiles to the floor, one by one. Use a utility knife to cut the tiles near walls and corners, as needed. You may need to use a heavy roller to ensure that the tiles stay in place.
- Clean the floor surface with a slightly damp cloth to remove any adhesive. Stay off the new floor for three days to let the adhesive stick properly.
- Laying vinyl sheets is similar, except that it's a lot more hard work: you need to cut the flooring to size, mix up adhesive, and then get to work.

SMART TIPS

- Wash spills on marble and limestone tiles with warm water. Add a little cleaning fluid to get rid of grease, and wipe clean with a damp cloth. Never use acidic substances such as vinegar or citric acid on marble, limestone, or natural stone floors or tiles.

- Wipe down hard water stains from ceramic tiles with vinegar. This dissolves the mineral build-up and can be wiped clean. Don't use abrasive cleaners or scouring powders; they can leave behind scratches.
- Use a solution of warm water and a few drops of dishwashing soap to clean terracotta tiles. Stay away from cleaners with acids, vinegar, or ammonia as these may damage or discolour the terracotta.
- Grout, which holds your tiles together, can become very dirty. Keep it clean with a mix of half cup baking soda, a quarter cup hydrogen peroxide, and 1 teaspoon dish soap. Coat the grout, let it sit for 10 minutes, and scrub with an old toothbrush.
- Wooden floors have a classy look, so it is important to keep them in top shape. Sweep daily, vacuum weekly, and wipe spills immediately. Wet mopping is a NO-NO – once a month with a really wrung-out mop will do.
- Nourish wooden floors once a month with a homemade polish: four tablespoons olive oil, 1 tablespoon vinegar, 2 cups of warm water, and a few drops of lemon essential oil. Buff till the floor shines!
- A crack in a tile can look ugly. Clean the crack (if it's a big one), fill in with epoxy or M-seal, and level with an ice-cream stick/toothpick. Let the material cure and apply some urethane-based paint in the tile colour.

15.

ALL-PURPOSE CLEANER

Everyone needs a jack-of-all-trades cleaner to banish dirt, grease, stubborn stains on glass and counters, and more. This is a simple recipe to create a cleaner that lasts almost forever.

What you need **Time** < 10 minutes

- ✓ 1 cup white vinegar
- ✓ 2 tbsps baking soda
- ✓ 2-3 drops lemon/lavender essential oil
- ✓ 3 cups warm water

How

- Mix the vinegar, essential oil, and a little water in a spray bottle.
- Add the baking soda and shake till it dissolves.
- Top with warm water. Shake, spray and clean.

Vinegar Baking Soda Oil Water

16.

UPHOLSTERY SPRAY

Thinking of calling an expert to 'shampoo' your sofa set? You may not need to if you use this spray solution regularly. Bonus: it also leaves your seating space smelling great!

What you need **Time** < 10 minutes

✓ 3-4 tbsps baking soda

✓ 2-3 drops lavender/orange essential oil

✓ 2 glasses warm water

How

- Mix the baking soda with the warm water till it dissolves completely.
- Add the essential oil and pour the mixture into a spray bottle.
- Spray the mixture on jaded, dull upholstery and scruff it up a bit to see it revive.
- For deep-set stains, mix together equal parts baking soda and water, and dab. Let sit for 15-20 minutes and vacuum up.

STAIN REMOVAL GUIDE

IF YOU GET THESE STAINS	REMOVE WITH THESE	IF YOU GET THESE STAINS	REMOVE WITH THESE
 Red wine	Salt + club soda	 Tea	Dish soap + vinegar + water
 Ink	Rubbing alcohol	 Chocolate	Dish soap + water
 Lipstick	Rubbing alcohol	 Tomato	Vinegar + water
 Makeup	Shaving cream	 Oil	Dish soap + hot water
 Deodorant	Lemon juice	 Blood	Salt water/ hydrogen peroxide
 Coffee	Baking soda + cold water		

17.

WOOD POLISHING SPRAY

Regular cleaning sprays don't work as well on wood, which needs a bit more nourishment and TLC. A dash of oil can help prime wood and keep it in good condition, and this DIY recipe marries that with the cleansing power of vinegar.

What you need **Time** < 10 minutes

✓ ¾ cup olive oil

✓ ¼ cup white vinegar

✓ 25-30 drops essential oil of your choice

How

- Pour all the ingredients into a small spray bottle and shake vigorously.
- To use, spray directly on wood furniture and buff with a clean, dry cloth. Shake forcefully before use each time to mix ingredients.

18.

SCREEN CLEANER

It isn't an exaggeration that we can't do without screens. From the phone to the laptop, and the TV to the desktop ... How can we survive without them? Keep all screens spotless and streak-free with this homemade cleaner.

What you need **Time < 10 minutes**

✓ ½ cup white vinegar
✓ ½ cup distilled water
✓ 2-3 drops lime essential oil

How

- Mix all the ingredients in a small spray bottle. The vinegar cleans surfaces to a shine and kills bacteria, while the addition of distilled water (can be replaced with boiled and strained water) ensures no streaks. Lemon oil, apart from smelling great, cuts oily residue and removes smudges.
- Spray on to a microfibre cloth and wipe surfaces down.

BONUS HACK

AIR FRESHENER

Who wants to walk into a room that reeks of last night's culinary excesses? An air freshener can mask unpleasant odours and create a pleasant environment. However, store-bought fresheners are full of chemicals. Say buh-bye to them and hello to a natural fragrance of your choosing.

What you need **Time < 10 minutes**

- ✓ 15-20 drops essential oil of your choice
- ✓ 1 cup white vinegar
- ✓ 1.5 cups water

How

- Mix white vinegar and water in a spray bottle, and shake vigorously.
- Add your favourite essential oil to make your home smell so fragrant and attractive that you wouldn't want to leave. Lemon, orange, lavender, neroli, cinnamon, and vanilla – they all smell divine!
- Shake the bottle well before using.

19.

LAUNDRY POWDER

Making your own laundry detergent is not something everyone does, which is surprising given how easy it is. Create this powder that's cheap and cleans just as efficiently as big brands.

What you need

- ✓ 200 gm Castile soap
- ✓ 2 cups baking soda
- ✓ 1 cup washing soda
- ✓ 25-30 drops essential oil of your choice
- ✓ 1 cup borax
- ✓ Grater/mixer

Time < 30 minutes

How

- Use a hand-held grater to grate the bar of soap into fine powder. You can also run it through a mixer.
- Old and dry soap creates finer power. Put the powder in a bowl, add all the other dry ingredients, and mix.
- Tip in the essential oil.
- Break up any lumps with your hands and store in an airtight container. A scoop should suffice for one wash load.

EXPERT CLEANING TIPS

- A water-and-vinegar solution and a sock on one hand can help clean blinds, louvers, shelves, and more.
- Give stainless steel appliances a super shine by buffing with some rubbing alcohol/olive oil and a microfibre cloth.
- Equal parts of vinegar and dish soap are an easy way to remove soap scum and grime that collect inside the shower and bath tub.
- Grab the atta resting in the fridge or a piece of bread to pick up tiny shards of glass. Move around the area to pick up all the itty-bitty pieces.
- Apply a generous dab of liquid hand soap to fabric stains, and let sit for up to 5 hours. Wash off. This hack will remove almost all food stains from clothes.
- Make a paste of baking soda and hydrogen peroxide. This is a miracle cleaner, and can clean every surface in your bathroom, kitchen, and balconies.
- The best way to vacuum a room? Begin with all horizontal surfaces and then move vertically to get rid of all trapped dirt and dust.
- Make your Swiffer-style sweeper floor mop do double duty by covering it with an old sock and using it to dust interior walls.
- Can't find the dustpan? Cut a deep paper plate or aluminium food pack into half and press into use.
- Wrap duct tape around a brush or paint roller, sticky side out, and run over furniture and carpets to pick up pet hair.
- Use a liquid toilet bowl cleaner and toilet brush to clean the inside of a dirty trash can thoroughly.
- Run a dry microfibre cloth over mirrors, countertops, and even tiles and fixtures to get a glazed finish.
- A whitening toothpaste and an old toothbrush can help clean grout.

20.

TOILET CLEANSER

Cleaning the toilet is a task that everyone hates, but no one can avoid. Make it fun by creating these bath bomb–style toilet cleaners that fizz, clean, and leave behind a sparkling bowl. Even kids will line up for toilet-cleaning duty!

What you need **Time < 15 minutes**

✓ 2 cups baking soda
✓ ½ cup citric acid
✓ 5 tbsps liquid Castile soap
✓ 2-3 drops essential oil of your choice
✓ Moulds of your choice

How

- Combine the baking soda and citric acid in a bowl.
- Add the Castile soap, a vegan, cruelty-free alternative to traditional tallow-based soaps.
- Drop in the essential oil and mix.
- Divide and place the mixture – it should look like damp sand – into a silicone mould.

- Let dry, remove, and store in an airtight container.
- When it's toilet-cleaning time, drop one bomb into the bowl, let it fizz, scrub with a brush, and flush!

SMART TIPS

- Soak a paper towel or cotton in vinegar or lemon juice, and wipe down the faucet to get rid of calcium, lime, and rust deposits.
- For more stubborn deposits, wrap the towel/cotton around problem areas and let sit for a few hours. Wipe clean.
- For adamant deposits, fill a plastic bag with vinegar and tie around the showerhead/faucet and let sit overnight.

BONUS HACK

FABRIC SOFTENER

The last addition to the wash cycle is a good-to-have, not a must-have. *Why spend the money if it's not really needed,* is what most of us think. Whipping it up at home lets you replicate the results of store-bought fabric softener at less than half the cost.

What you need **Time** < 10 minutes

✓ 5 cups water

✓ 500 ml (bottle) hair conditioner

✓ 2 cups vinegar

✓ 2-3 drops lavender essential oil (optional)

How

- Put all the ingredients in a large vessel and mix thoroughly – a whisk does this job admirably. There's no need to splash out on expensive conditioners; the most basic and cheapest one will do.
- Let it sit for 10 minutes and pour into old, plastic bottles.
- Use about a quarter cup for every wash load for fragrant, soft clothes.

THE COMPLETE CLEANING CHECKLIST

Every Day

- Make bed
- Dust regular-use surfaces
- Clean dirty dishes
- Do laundry
- Clean gas
- Sweep and mop floors
- Wipe down bathroom surfaces
- Sanitize kitchen and bathroom sinks
- Wash kitchen cloths

Every Week

- Wipe down furniture
- Dust picture frames/accents
- Change bedding
- Clean microwave
- Wipe down kitchen appliances
- Bin expired food
- Wash bathrooms
- Clean mirrors
- Wash foot mats
- Wash dust bins

Every Month

- Descale electric kettle
- Bring down cobwebs
- Dust doors and door frames
- Clean under and behind furniture
- Clean light fixtures and fans
- Wipe down walls
- Clear refrigerator
- Deep clean gas burners
- Clean washing machine
- Wash shower curtains
- Clean verandahs/outside furniture

Every Six Months

- Wash pillows
- Clean ovens
- Clean out freezer
- Wash curtains
- Deep clean windows
- Deep clean carpet/upholstery
- Clean AC filters
- Sort clothes
- Arrange pantry

21.

NATURAL BUG REPELLENT

This homemade bug spray is easy to put together and easier to use – inside and outside the house. The use of different kinds of essential oils helps get rid of varied bugs and insects – and ensures a great fragrance!

What you need **Time** < **10 minutes**

- ✓ 2 cups white vinegar
- ✓ 2 cups distilled water
- ✓ 10-12 drops lavender essential oil
- ✓ 10-12 drops lemon eucalyptus essential oil
- ✓ 10-12 drops citronella essential oil

How

- Mix the vinegar and distilled water in a spray bottle, and tip in the essential oils.
- Shake gently to mix and spray liberally as an indoor/outdoor bug repellent.

22.

ANTI-BUG SKIN SPRAY

Citronella or lemon essential oils work well when diluted with a carrier oil to repel bugs. But there's no need to fear if you don't have a stock of essential oils. This easy DIY method uses a few herbs and vodka to make a bug spray that works almost as well on skin.

What you need **Time** < 30 minutes

✓ 1.5 cups distilled water
✓ ½ cup vodka
✓ ½ cup dried herbs (peppermint, lemongrass, lavender, rosemary)
✓ 5-8 cloves

How

- Boil the water, and tip in the herbs and cloves.
- Let it simmer for 2-3 minutes, mix well, and turn off the gas. Cover and let cool.
- Strain the mixture and mix the water with the alcohol.
- Pour into a spray bottle, store in a cool place and spray on skin when needed.

BONUS HACK

MOSQUITO REPELLENT CANDLE

This DIY packs a double punch: it looks super-pretty and keeps mosquitoes at bay. It's ideal for use in verandahs, balconies, and during outdoor parties and get-togethers.

What you need

- ✓ 1 glass jar
- ✓ 2 lemons (sliced)
- ✓ 3-4 rosemary sprigs
- ✓ 6-8 lemongrass strips
- ✓ 10-15 drops eucalyptus essential oil
- ✓ 1 floating candle

Time < **10 minutes**

How

- Place the lemon slices, rosemary sprigs, and lemongrass strips in the jar, and drip in the essential oil.
- Fill the jar with water up to the mouth.
- Float the candle in water and light it.

23.

HOMEMADE PESTICIDE

Growing garlic in your garden is a good way to keep plant pests and bugs away, but what if you can't grow your own garlic? You can use garlic pods to make your own natural insecticide and keep your plants verdant and green.

What you need **Time** < **15 minutes**

✓ 20-25 garlic cloves (peeled)

✓ 1 cup mint, both leaves and stems (chopped)

✓ 1 tbsp oil

✓ 2 tsps cayenne pepper

✓ 2 litres water

How

- Blitz the garlic and mint to a fine paste.
- Transfer the mixture to a large saucepan, add water and cayenne pepper, and bring to a rolling boil.
- Remove from heat, stir in the oil, and let sit overnight.
- Strain into spray bottles. Shake well before using and spray affected plants, including the undersides of the leaves. One application may be enough, but spray again, if needed.

ESSENTIAL OILS – HERE'S WHY!

Use a few drops of these oils to get rid of a variety of insects and bugs.

- **Citrus:** Bugs, fleas, aphids, mites, and flies
- **Garlic:** Ticks
- **Lemon eucalyptus:** Mosquitoes
- **Thyme:** Mosquitoes
- **Cinnamon:** Mosquitoes
- **Lavender:** Mosquitoes
- **Peppermint:** Mosquitoes
- **Dill:** Cockroaches

BYE-BYE BUGS

- A small amount of Vicks VapoRub rubbed on to the skin acts as a mosquito repellent.
- Mix neem oil and coconut oil in equal proportions, and use liberally on body. Adieu, mosquitoes!
- Dip a cotton pad in a mix of sugar, borax, and warm water to draw out ants from their hiding places.
- Sprinkle cinnamon powder/black pepper on the points of entry of ants to ban them from your kitchen.
- Mix apple cider vinegar with liquid dish soap to create a natural trap for fruit flies.
- Spray wall corners and the outdoor areas with a mix of half cup soap and 2 litres water to bid adieu to spiders.
- Sprinkle boric acid in corners, under sinks, and other problem areas to get rid of cockroaches.

- Bay leaves work as natural cockroach repellents.
- Chopped onion and a teaspoon of baking soda placed at strategic corners can also keep your home roach-free.
- Hang a bough of fresh mint in the kitchen to repel flies. Sachets of crushed mint work well in other areas.
- Burn sage or rosemary to keep flying insects away.
- A pomander – a lemon studded with cloves – strung up in the kitchen keeps flies and mosquitoes at bay.
- Plant basil in containers, and place them in the kitchen to repel flies and mosquitoes.

- Dab neem oil in corners and crevices to keep most bugs and insects away.
- Drop a couple of cloves or a bay leaf into your rice, wheat, and flour bins to keep weevils out.
- Moths have a natural aversion to cedar, so slip some rice grains into small cloth bags and add a few drops of the essential oil to create DIY scented sachets.

24.

FIX A FLAT TYRE

Being stuck with a dead cellphone and a flat tyre may lead you to berate yourself, but that won't be enough in a roadside emergency. A flat tyre can happen at any time, any place, and it's important for any driver to know how to deal with it.

What you need **Time** < 45 minutes

- ✓ Jack
- ✓ Lug wrench
- ✓ Flashlight
- ✓ Small cut of wood (2x6 inches)
- ✓ Wheel wedges
- ✓ Inflated spare tyre

How

- Drive into a safe, level stretch of road and turn on the hazard lights (blinkers). Pull up the handbrake and position the wheel wedges (if you don't have them, can use large stones) in front of (if you're changing the rear tyre) or behind the tyres (if fixing a flat at the front). This ensures the car doesn't roll while you're at work.

- If your vehicle has a hubcap, remove with the flat end of the lug wrench. Turn the lug nuts anti-clockwise until you feel them give – you may need to throw all your body weight against them by foot. Loosen, but don't remove yet.
- Slide the jack in beneath the vehicle frame alongside the flat. You may want to follow the instructions for jack placement in your car manual to raise safely. Place a small cut of wood beneath the jack – this ensures it doesn't settle under the weight of your car. Raise the car until the flat tyre is six inches off the ground.
- Remove the lug nuts and pull the tyre off gently. Line up the rim of the spare tyre with the lug bolts and place. Put the lug nuts back on and tighten by hand. Use the jack and lower the vehicle; the spare should almost be on the ground. Use the wrench to tighten the lug nuts, turning clockwise till they are as tight as possible.
- Lower the vehicle till it touches the ground and remove the jack. Put the hubcap back in place, remove and stow all equipment into the boot, and drop the flat tyre off at a garage to get it fixed.

25.

JUMP-START A CAR

A dead car battery can leave you stranded on the road or highway. Knowing how to jump-start – or boost - a car is a life skill that anyone who drives should learn. Find someone who's happy to help and has a car with a fully charged battery. Keep jump leads in your car for such emergencies.

What you need

✓ Jump cables

✓ A good Samaritan

How

- Park both cars as near as possible without touching, so their batteries are within easy reach. Pull up the handbrake and turn off the ignition.
- Use the red jump lead to connect the working battery's positive terminal to the flat battery's positive terminal. Take the black jump lead and attach the negative end to the negative terminal on the working battery. Fix the other end to an earthing point

(unpainted metal on the engine block or chassis) away from the flat battery and fuel system.

- After five minutes of making the connections, start the working car's engine and let it run for a minute or so. Turn on the engine in your car (that has a flat battery). Let both cars run and idle, at a fast pace, for about 10 minutes.
- Turn off both car engines and carefully disconnect the leads. Go in the reverse order – compared to the way they were connected. Remove the black lead from your car first and then the red lead from the good Samaritan's car. Don't let the leads touch each other or the cars as you disconnect and remove them.
- Turn the keys in the ignition to see if your car starts. If it doesn't, there may be another problem and you'll have to call for highway/road assistance or your mechanic. It's important to remember that batteries produce flammable gases. Never try to jump-start a battery that looks damaged or is leaking, and don't use damaged jump leads.

SECTION 2

FOOD AND KITCHEN

'Happiness is a small house, with a big kitchen.'

—Alfred Hitchcock

A bowl of piping hot rajma chawal, puran poli dripping with ghee, oh-so-spicy bhel, a slice of pizza bursting with cheese, a brownie that crumbles the moment you stick a spoon into it, a big bowl of ice cream topped with sprinkles ...

It's a no-brainer, really!

Food = happiness.

For the longest time, I thought food-related happiness was synonymous with an indulgent meal in a fancy-schmancy restaurant. Eons seem to have passed since that thought took root in my mind. Adulting has taught me a vital life lesson: happiness is, more often than not, homemade.

I now know that happiness lies in the small things: a flickering candle, a glass of wine, the aroma of a chocolate cake baking in the oven, a meal put together from scratch, or the fragrance from a stovetop potpourri wafting across the home. It's not for nothing that the kitchen is called the heart of the home.

Everything happens in the kitchen; life happens in the kitchen.

This is a room that wears many hats – it acts as your workplace, computer room, entertainment centre, bill kiosk, study room, yoga area, and, of course, the cooking zone where you dish up delicious, nutritious food, and hang with family and friends.

Time spent in the kitchen, cooking to satisfy the tongue's need for taste and the body's need for food, can help nurture the mind and promote mental well-being. Multiple studies have revealed that cooking is associated with life satisfaction and is the best predictor of subjective happiness. Cooking has multiple benefits: it keeps you healthy, is creative, calms you down, helps enhance connections, improves your quality of life, *and* saves money. And it's a life skill everyone must know.

But the busiest room in the house needs more than cooking to keep it in fine fettle; it needs to be organized and managed properly to ensure it stays in top working order. Make certain that you shop for staples in bulk and store them appropriately, organizing the contents of the cupboards and drawers (rule of thumb: like goes with like), routinely going through the contents, and putting in place a meal plan can make cooking easier.

Maintaining a high standard of hygiene and cleanliness is imperative, of course, and no kitchen can do without it!

KIT OUT YOUR PANTRY

'Laughter is brightest where food is best.'

—Old Irish proverb

Would you be able to cook at home, enjoy hygge (like we all aim to these days), and ensure laughter if homebound for a week, a month, or more?

We thought that hoarding food was for Neanderthals and the like, but the COVID-19 pandemic and the consequent lockdowns showed us how important it was to have a well-stocked pantry.

Apart from the sense of food security it provides, a kitted-out pantry makes meal planning and preparation easier. You can map out a weekly/monthly menu, prioritize unused and unprocessed ingredients, avoid sudden trips to the market for ingredients, simplify grocery shopping, and make cooking easier on yourself. A home pantry is also a great way to save money as you tap sales, buy in bulk, and make fewer shopping runs (reduced temptations and impulse buys!).

How long should your pantry help you subsist?

A small crisis could leave you without access to food supplies for two weeks while a long-term disaster could leave you stranded for anywhere between two and six months. It's a good idea to stay prepared for a mix of short and long-term emergencies.

While stocking up, remember that the shelf life of any food product is affected by oxygen, humidity, light, heat, bacteria, insects, and rodents. The simplest advice to extend the shelf life of all kinds of food is to keep it away from heat, light, moisture, and oxygen. The packaging also has a bearing on shelf life. For long-term food storage, foods such as grains, lentils, and sugar can be stored in packages where the oxygen is removed (some stores offer this service). These can often last in cool, dark locations for 10-15 years.

So, let's get started.

SERIOUS STAPLES

Everyone's essentials will vary based on preferences, budgets, and dietary restrictions. But there are some basics that ensure you cook with real and unprocessed ingredients, and dish out healthy meals – every single day.

PANTRY ESSENTIALS

Grains and Flour

- Rice
- Wheat
- Barley
- Corn
- Millet
- Buckwheat
- Wheat flour
- All-purpose flour

Lentils, Legumes, Pulses

- Chole
- Chana
- Rajma
- Lobia
- Green moong
- Whole black urad dal
- Split urad dal
- Yellow moong dal
- Arhar dal
- Chana dal
- Dehydrated green/white peas

Herbs, Spices, Oils

- Turmeric
- Red chilli powder
- Cumin seeds
- Clove
- Cardamom
- Pepper
- Coriander seeds
- Nutmeg
- Mustard seeds
- Fenugreek seeds
- Cinnamon
- Chilli flakes
- Bay leaves
- Cooking oil, of your choice
- Coconut oil
- Ghee

Miscellaneous

- Coffee
- Tea
- Cocoa
- Sugar
- Salt
- Honey
- Dried fruit, nuts, and seeds
- Butter
- Cheese
- Milk powder
- Pasta/noodles
- Cereals
- Oats
- Vinegar
- Baking soda
- Baking powder
- Yeast
- Comfort food (cookies, candy bars, chocolate, and namkeens)
- Jams and preserves
- Ketchup, mayo, and mustard
- Pickles and sauces

What should you aim for? A balanced mix that helps you prepare routine meals, comfort foods, and treats. The table on the previous page can also double up as your monthly grocery shopping checklist.

STORING YOUR STAPLES

Moisture and heat are food storage's greatest enemy. Plan your pantry such that you can deal with these threats and store your staples for longer.

- Onions can last for months if stored the right way. Cut up a pantyhose, toss an onion into the feet side, and tie a knot. Place another onion above the knot and continue, until you have a line of onions. Hang in a cool, dark, and dry place to keep the air circulating and banish the growth of mould.
- Potatoes survive for weeks if you keep them in a low-moisture, cool environment such as a dark cupboard. Place an apple in the basket to keep them from sprouting eyes.
- The US National Honey Board says honey can last decades or even centuries if stored properly. Store the golden liquid in a sealed glass container in a cool, dark place. Pop the jar into warm water to reverse any crystallization (it's normal).
- The best way to keep rice and grains safe from rodents, pests, and insects is to store them in airtight containers, be it wooden barrels, plastic cartons, or glass jars. Add a few neem or bay leaves to prevent bug attacks.
- Salt can last up to 10 years if stored properly. Keep it in a cool and dark place in a glass container, and toss in a few cloves to

prevent clumping. Seal the container with a plastic lid, for the corrosive nature of salt can eat away a metal lid.

- Sugar can also be stored indefinitely if packed correctly. Pour into an airtight glass jar with a few grains of rice or a desiccant packet; these help absorb moisture and prevent clumping. Place in a cool, dark place.
- That brown sugar that you picked up for your baking binges will stay soft and scoopable if you store it in an airtight container, and toss in an orange peel.
- Dry-roasting pulses before storing them in glass jars can keep them fresh for longer. Toss a couple of dry red chillies into the jar to prevent spoilage.
- Keep bananas fresh for longer by wrapping the end of the bunch with plastic wrap. This blocks ethylene gases from releasing out of the stem, which causes the fruit to ripen quickly.
- Want to get your fresh produce – especially potatoes and root veggies – really clean before storing? Scrub with a mix of water and baking soda to remove soil, grime, and pesticides.
- Wipe down your pantry shelves with a disinfectant laced with clove oil to keep bugs and insects at bay.

SHELF LIFE: BEST BEFORE AND USE BY

Who hasn't given shelf life a thought or two? This is the specific time period during which food maintains acceptable characteristics under specified storage and handling conditions. Most packaged foods with a shelf life of less than two years have a 'best-before' or 'use-by' date stamped on the container.

One of the biggest misconceptions we have is that packaged food can't be consumed after the best-before date has passed. Reality check? It's just a recommendation!

Best-before date: This gives you an idea of how long the food item will last before it loses quality. Most manufacturers choose a best-before date well before the time when the food is expected to actually deteriorate and spoil. Consider this as a guide. If the food looks and smells as expected, it should be safe to eat – even if the best-before date has passed.

Use-by date: Foods that should not be consumed after a certain date for health and safety reasons tend to have a 'use-by' date. This date is a safety measure, and gives you an idea of when food could be potentially dangerous to eat. Keep an eye on high-risk foods such as meat, fish, eggs, and dairy, and toss out if the use-by date has passed. Do not consume even if it looks and smells fine.

26.

BANANA BREAD

It's a bread, it's a cake; no, it's both. There's something about banana bread – it makes your home smell heavenly when it's in the oven; it makes you feel content when it's buttered liberally and in your tummy. This easy-as-pie recipe can be put together by even a child, and lends itself well to big-batch baking and freezing.

What you need

- ✓ 1.5 cups all-purpose flour
- ✓ ¾ cup sugar
- ✓ 3 ripe mashed bananas
- ✓ 2 eggs (large)
- ✓ 1 tsp ground cinnamon
- ✓ 1 tsp baking soda
- ✓ ½ tsp baking powder
- ✓ ½ cup vegetable oil
- ✓ ½ tsp salt
- ✓ ¼ cup honey
- ✓ ¼ cup water

For topping

- ✓ 3 tbsps demerara sugar
- ✓ 1 tbsp ground cinnamon

Time < 2 hours

Makes 1 loaf

How

- Preheat the oven to 350°F (175°C). Butter and dot a 9x5-inch metal/silicon loaf pan with flour.

- Mix the flour, sugar, cinnamon, baking soda, baking powder, and salt. In another bowl, whisk the banana, eggs, oil, honey, and water. Mix the dry ingredients into the wet ones and pour into the loaf pan.
- Combine the topping ingredients in a small bowl and sprinkle evenly over the batter.
- Bake until a tester inserted into the centre comes out clean. This depends on the oven, but should take about 1 hour.
- Let sit outside for 30 minutes, and remove from pan. Cool completely before slicing.

27.

SANDWICH BREAD

Nothing says special more than the aroma of freshly baked bread rising in the oven. The perfect loaf of bread may seem like the holy grail of baking, but it's possible to turn out bread with a tender, soft interior and a crispy crust without going crazy about the ingredients, kneading, resting, rising, and more.

What you need

- ✓ 2¾ cups all-purpose flour (plus extra for kneading)
- ✓ 2¾ cups wholewheat flour
- ✓ 1 cup toned milk
- ✓ ¼ cup unflavoured honey
- ✓ 2 tbsps oil
- ✓ 1 tsp salt
- ✓ 2 tsps active dry yeast
- ✓ 1¼ cups warm water

Time < **3 hours**

Makes 2 **loaves**

How

- Pour the water into a bowl and add the yeast; let stand till the powder dissolves. Add the oil, milk, and honey, and mix. Tip in 2 cups of all-purpose flour and salt, and combine into the liquid mixture. Add the rest of the flours. Mix to create a loose dough and let rest for 20 minutes.

- Knead the dough till it is no longer sticky – like the atta put together for roti. Add extra flour, a spoonful at a time, if needed. Knead in a little oil and shape the dough into a ball. Cover the bowl and set aside for about 1.5 hours. It will rise to about double the size. Divide the dough into two balls and let it sit for 15 minutes.
- Grease two loaf pans (8x4 inches). Fold the balls of dough into two rectangular loaves, ensuring that the surface is taut. Set aside for about 45 minutes to let the loaves rise. Heat the oven to 425°F (220°C). Make a cut in the tops of the loaves and place in oven.
- Bake for 30-40 minutes after turning down the temperature to 375°F. The loaves will be golden brown and will sound hollow when done. Let cool before slicing. This bread can be stored for several days at room temperature and up to 3 months in the freezer.

28.

MOZZARELLA CHEESE

What would pizza be without those stretchy, stringy bites of mozzarella cheese? Elevate your pizza from good to great by garnishing it with fresh, homemade mozzarella. Apart from not having to rely on store-bought cheese any more, you also know it's fresh and additive/preservative-free.

What you need

✓ 3 litres full-cream milk
✓ ½ cup vinegar
✓ 1 tbsp salt
✓ Pot/pan for boiling

Time < 1 hour

Makes 400 gm

How

- Bring the full-cream milk to a gentle boil, stirring continuously. The milk should be lukewarm, about 115°F (45°C).
- Turn off the flame and stir as you add the vinegar. Over-stirring may break up the curds being formed. Cover and rest for 15-20 minutes. Drain the curds, reserving the whey, and squeeze the water out.

- Heat the whey, but make sure it doesn't boil, till about 80°C (175°F), and add the salt. Stir well and turn off the flame. Drop the soft cheesy ball into the whey water and keep for a minute. Remove, squeeze out extra water, and knead. Repeat five times or till the ball is soft. Overdoing this step may lead to rubbery cheese.
- Place the ball in ice water for 2 minutes to set the cheese completely. Wrap in cling film/beeswax paper and refrigerate for 2 hours. This can be used over the course of a week.

29.

FRUIT JAM

Hot buttered toast slathered with fruit jam = sweet dreams. The dreams get sweeter if the jam is homemade. Jam-making may seem to be a tedious process, but this simple method breaks it down into easy steps. This recipe works best with berries, but you can jam with other seasonal fruits as well. The secret is time: all mixes of fruit and sugar need time to cook and thicken.

What you need

- ✓ 5 cups fresh strawberries, plums, or peaches, chopped
- ✓ ¾ cup granulated sugar
- ✓ 2 tbsps lemon juice
- ✓ A pinch of salt
- ✓ A pinch of nutmeg

Time > 1 hour

Makes 2 jars, 225 gm each

How

- Prep the fruit. Discard the bruised sections and dice. Mix the fruit and sugar in a saucepan. At this time, place a few clean steel spoons in the freezer.

- Put the fruit-sugar mix in a heavy-bottomed utensil, and add the lemon juice and salt. Place over a medium flame and mash the fruit with a potato masher till it's chunky.
- Bring the mixture to a boil, stirring frequently. Add the nutmeg powder and continue to boil, stirring frequently. The fruit appears chunky and jammy after about 20 minutes. Peaches and plums may take longer.
- To check if the jam is ready, get a spoon from the freezer and scoop up a bit of the mixture. Run a finger through it after a few seconds. If it leaves a distinct track, it's ready. If not, keep cooking and check again later.

- Turn off the heat, cool the mix and carefully transfer into clean jars that have been rinsed with boiling hot water. Cool to room temperature and seal. Store in the refrigerator for up to 3 weeks or freeze for up to 3 months.

30.

HOMEMADE MAYONNAISE

A burger ain't a burger without a dollop of mayo. The condiment is credited to the French chef of the Duke de Richelieu while creating a victory feast in 1756, but the claim is disputed.

What you need

- ✓ 1 egg (cold from the refrigerator)
- ✓ ¾ cup oil (cooled in the refrigerator)
- ✓ 1 tbsp lemon juice
- ✓ ¼ tbsp salt
- ✓ 1 tsp mustard

Time < 15 minutes

Makes 1 cup

How

- Put all five ingredients into a tall container in this order: egg, oil, lemon juice, salt, and mustard.
- Use your immersion blender at the highest speed, without moving it for 15-20 seconds. You will see the mixture emulsifying soon.
- Move the blender up and down to ensure that the mixture is homogenous. Refrigerate in a glass jar. It will last a week in the fridge.

KITCHEN CONVERSIONS

Kitchen conversions are always baffling. How many teaspoons is one cup and vice-versa? What is one tablespoon in teaspoons? We have you covered.

Dry measures

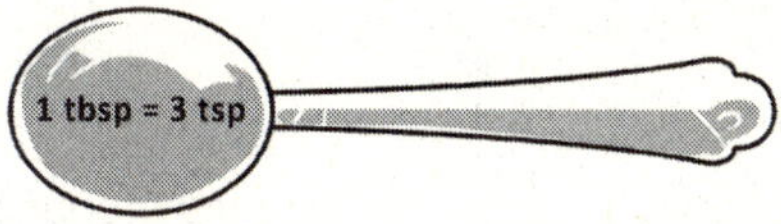

Wet measures

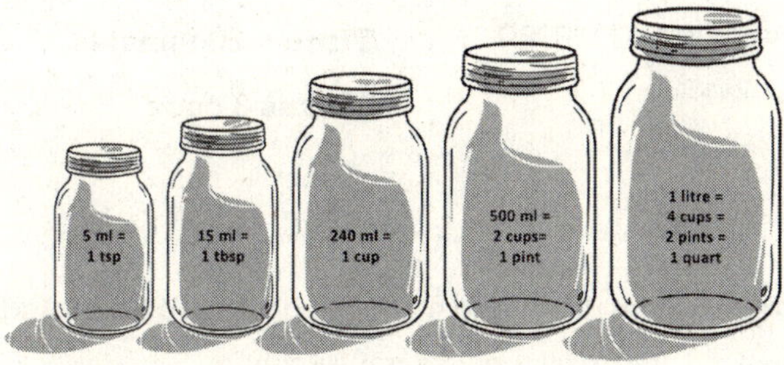

31.

PIZZA AND PASTA SAUCE

There are always going to be evenings when your menu plan falls apart. Instead of getting takeaway, make and store this simple tomato-based sauce that you can use on pizzas, pastas, bread/ roti pizzas, and more. Traditionally, pasta sauce is slow simmered while pizza sauce isn't cooked, but this recipe takes a middle path. Bonus: It can also be used for Indian curries if you add spice powders and tadka!

What you need

- ✓ 4 tomatoes (finely chopped)
- ✓ 1 onion (finely chopped)
- ✓ 2 tbsps olive oil
- ✓ 2 garlic cloves (minced)
- ✓ 1 tsp sugar
- ✓ 1 tbsp basil
- ✓ 1 tsp oregano
- ✓ 2 tbsps cheese (grated)
- ✓ 1 cup water
- ✓ Salt and pepper (to taste)

Time < 20 minutes

Makes 3 cups

How

- In a kadhai, heat the oil and sauté the garlic till golden. Add the onions and stir-fry till they are translucent.

- Add the tomatoes, sugar, oregano, basil, and a cup of water. Let it come to a boil. Add the cheese, and season with salt and pepper. Simmer for 10 minutes.
- Blitz the mix in your blender when cool. You can keep it a bit chunky or make it real smooth. Store in a resealable container and refrigerate for up to a week, or freeze the sauce in ice-cube trays and then store the cubes for up to three months.

32.

PASTA FROM SCRATCH

Most of us know that pasta is of Italian descent, but did you know that almost every country has its own version? Germany and Hungary swear by spaetzle. Poland has the pierogi, Greece enjoys the orzo, and what is dal dhokli but an Indianized version of pasta? What do you do when your homemade sauce is ready, but there's no pasta at hand? You make it!

What you need

- ✓ 1½ cups wholewheat flour
- ✓ 1½ cups all-purpose flour
- ✓ 4 eggs (at room temperature)
- ✓ A pinch of baking soda
- ✓ ½ tsp salt
- ✓ Water

Time < 30 minutes

Makes 6 servings

How

- Combine the wholewheat flour, all-purpose flour, salt, and baking soda in a *paraat*.

- Make a well in the centre of the mound of flour and crack all the eggs into it. Use a light hand to break the eggs up and combine the flour mix. Keep kneading till all flour is absorbed and the dough begins to take s'
- Bind the dough together till smooth (like roti atta). Add water if it seems dry and form a ball. Wrap in a piece of cloth and refrigerate for an hour.

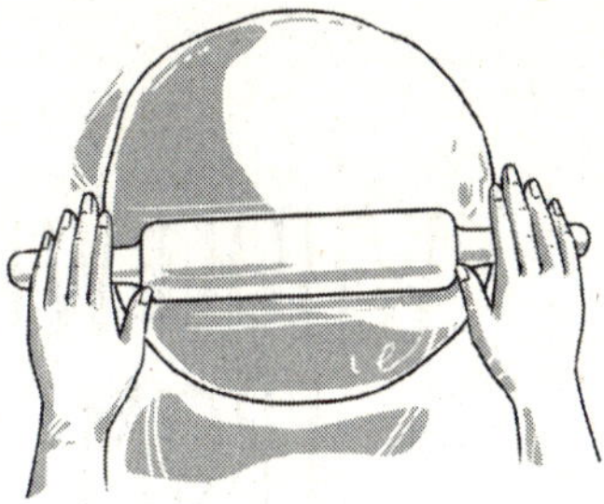

- Remove the dough and section into four parts. Flour the *patla*, or platform, and roll out one ball of dough at a time into as-thin-as-you-can-make-the rotis (aim for rectangular).

- Fold the rotis over several times and cut the roll into 0.75 cm thick strips of fettuccine pasta. Dust some flour over the strips and untangle them. Repeat with the rest of the dough.

- Cook in boiling salted water till tender; it takes less than three minutes. Strain and serve as you like. Freeze in small nests (for up to two months) and pop into boiling water to cook. The pasta's done when it floats to the surface.

33.

WHOLEWHEAT PIZZA FROM SCRATCH

You can't get a great pizza without a strong foundation: the dough. Whatever your preference may be – thin and crisp or thick and chewy – this lean dough recipe promises the right texture and flavour. The best part? This from-scratch crust is made of 100 per cent wholewheat. So, pizza = healthy.

What you need

- ✓ 3¼ cups wholewheat flour
- ✓ 1 tbsp yeast
- ✓ 1 tbsp olive oil (and a drop to brush crust)
- ✓ 1 tbsp honey
- ✓ 1 tbsp salt
- ✓ Pizza sauce, as needed (See Hack 31)
- ✓ Toppings of choice

Time < 2.5 hours

Makes 2, 12-inch pizzas

How

- Prepare the yeast according to the instructions on the packet. Add the olive oil, honey, and salt. Mix in 3 cups of flour with a large spatula till the dough starts to form.

- Knead by hand on a lightly floured surface till it forms a smooth and elastic dough. If the dough seems sticky, add up to a quarter cup more whole wheat flour. Your dough is ready if it bounces back when you poke it.
- Coat a large bowl with olive oil and run the ball-shaped dough over the surface so that it's coated on all sides. Cover tightly with plastic wrap and allow to rise for about 1.5 hours.
- Punch the dough once to release air and separate into two balls. Let the two balls rest in separate bowls, covered with wrap, for 20 minutes. You can freeze one ball after this in case you want to make only one pizza.
- Preheat the oven to 475°F (245°C) and let it heat for 30 minutes. Grease and dust two baking sheets, and sprinkle with flour. Flatten each ball into an approximately 12-inch roundel and lift up the edge of the dough to create a lip.
- Brush the top lightly with olive oil to prevent the filling from making your pizza crust soggy. Push small dents into the surface of the dough with your fingers to prevent bubbling. Transfer dough to the baking sheet gently.
- Top with the sauce, cheese, and your choice of toppings such as vegetables, chicken strips, pepperoni, and more. Bake for 15 minutes or until the cheese has melted and the crust is light brown.
- Slice the pizza and serve hot. Store leftover pizza in an airtight container in the refrigerator for a couple of days. Baked pizza slices can be frozen up to a month.

34.

MULTIPURPOSE GRAVY

The hectic millennial life doesn't leave much time for chopping and sautéing. What if you could cut your cooking time by making a large batch of multipurpose gravy? Freeze in usable portion sizes and make whatever you want – chole, rajma, alu matar, egg curry, mix veg gravy, and more. What else could you ask for!

What you need

- ✓ 6 onions (large)
- ✓ 8 tomatoes (medium)
- ✓ 10-12 garlic cloves
- ✓ Ginger root (3-inch piece)
- ✓ ½ tsp haldi
- ✓ 2 tsps cumin seeds
- ✓ 1 large piece cinnamon
- ✓ 3-4 cloves
- ✓ 2 bay leaves
- ✓ Salt to taste
- ✓ ½ cup oil

Time < 1 hour

Makes 2, 250-gm jars

How

- Heat oil in a heavy-bottomed pan and toss in the cumin seeds and haldi. Stir in the roughly chopped onions, garlic, and ginger.

Cook on a medium flame until the onion becomes translucent. Add the bay leaves, cloves, cinnamon stick, and stir.

- Chop the tomatoes and add to the onion mix. Cook for roughly 15-20 minutes till the mixture becomes mushy and oil starts to separate from the masala. Keep stirring in between, every 5 minutes or so.
- Switch off the gas and allow the mixture to cool. Remove the cinnamon stick and bay leaves. Blend the mixture, add salt, and store in airtight containers in the refrigerator. Freeze for up to six months.

BONUS HACK

MIXED VEGETABLE PICKLE

Come winter, and we all turn to mums, aunts, or nanis with only one request: a bottle of their crunchy, tangy gobhi-shalgam-gajar aachar. Be it piping hot parathas, homely dal-chawal, or pulao and raita, this pickle enhances flavours and is sure to leave you licking your fingers.

What you need

- ✓ 300 gms turnip (peeled and sliced)
- ✓ 300 gms cauliflower (cut into florets)
- ✓ 300 gms carrots (peeled and sliced)
- ✓ 8 garlic cloves (crushed)
- ✓ 300 ml mustard oil
- ✓ 1 tsp chilli powder
- ✓ 60 gms mustard seeds (ground)
- ✓ ½ tsp turmeric powder
- ✓ ½ tsp asafoetida
- ✓ 3.5 tbsps salt

Time > 2 days

Makes 20 servings

How

- Heat water in a large saucepan. Add the veggies when the water comes to a boil and cook for 3-4 minutes. Drain and pour cold water over the vegetables. Lay them on a clean cloth and let dry for 4-5 hours.

- Scatter the ground mustard seeds, chilli powder, turmeric powder, asafoetida, salt, and garlic over the vegetables. Empty the mixture into a clean, sterilized glass jar/ceramic *barni*.
- Heat mustard oil till it starts to smoke. Remove from heat and let cool. Pour the lukewarm oil into the jar. Place in the sun for 2 days and shake the jar twice every day. The pickle is ready in 2 days. It can be stored in a cool and dry place for up to 3-5 months.

35.

HOMEMADE BUTTER AND GHEE

We Indians love our ghee – on rotis and parathas, on freshly steamed rice, and in dal tadka. But most of us desisted from consuming it till celeb nutritionist Rujuta Divekar recommended it – and how! Forget the store-bought version and make your own aromatic ghee by rounding up malai, making makhan, and boiling to eliminate proteins and milk solids. The reward: clarified butter.

What you need

✓ 1 large jar of milk cream

✓ 2 tbsps yoghurt

Time > 1 hour

Makes 500 gm

How

- Every day, skim the malai from the top of milk after boiling and collect in an airtight container. Keep collecting for about a month or so, and keep frozen. Remove and let stand till the cream comes to room temperature, add a couple of tablespoons of dahi to the mix, and let it stand overnight.

- Add a glass of ice-cold water to the container and churn using the traditional Indian wooden whisk – I'm just joking! Your hand blender will do just fine! The butter will separate; form it into a ball with your hand and wash with drinking water. The buttermilk can be used to bind flour into a dough. This butter can be used as is (store in refrigerator for a month) or converted into ghee.
- To make ghee, place the butter into a large kadhai and melt completely. Stir regularly till the butter changes colour and looks frothy. Continue till the milk solids gather at the bottom and the bubbles turn transparent. Boil till the liquid turns golden brown and aromatic. Let cool and filter the ghee.

36.

FREEZE VEGETABLES

When you're short on time and hunger strikes, frozen vegetables can be your best friend. Veggies are blanched – in boiling water or steam for a short period of time – to slow the action of enzymes that cause loss of flavour, texture, and colour, and then frozen. Stored in different bags, they make cooking easy-peasy and let you put out a proper meal quickly. Bonus tip: Toss these into the multipurpose gravy (See Hack 34) for a quick meal.

What you need **Time > 1 hour**

- ✓ 2 litres water (1 litre for ½ kg veggies)
- ✓ 1 kg vegetables of your choice

How

- Put the chopped veggies – carrots, broccoli, peas, or others – in a steel sieve and fit into a large pot with a lid. Use one litre of water for half a kg of veggies. Lower into vigorously boiling water and place the lid. Keep the heat high. Blanching removes dirt and organisms, brightens the colour, and stems the loss of vitamins.

- Always blanch only for the suggested time (2-3 minutes). Under-blanching stimulates the activity of enzymes and is worse than not blanching at all. Over-blanching leads to a loss of flavour, colour, vitamins, and minerals.
- As soon as the blanching is complete, cool the vegetables quickly and thoroughly to stop the cooking process. Plunge the basket of vegetables into a large quantity of cold water, 15°C or below. Change the water frequently, if possible.
- Put the blanched and drained vegetables into meal-size freezer bags or containers. Pack tightly so there's no air locked in. Leave a half-inch headspace at the top of the containers and close. Fill freezer bags within three inches of the top. This leaves space for the food to expand. Label with the name and freezing date.

BONUS HACK

EASY KIMCHI

K for Korea, K for kimchi. This Korean staple is a traditional side dish of salted and fermented vegetables, including cabbage, radish, spring onions, celery, garlic, ginger, and more. And with more of us getting acquainted with Korean culture, courtesy K-dramas, K-pop, and K-beauty, it makes sense to dish up your own kimchi, and enjoy health benefits such as improved digestion, better immunity, and increased weight loss.

What you need

- ✓ 1 green cabbage
- ✓ ¼ cup iodine-free sea/plain salt
- ✓ Water (filtered)
- ✓ 5-6 cloves of garlic
- ✓ 3-inch strip of ginger
- ✓ 2 tbsps fish sauce (or 3 tbsps water for veg kimchi)
- ✓ 1 tsp granulated sugar
- ✓ 1-5 tbsps red chilli flakes
- ✓ 1 tsp black peppercorns
- ✓ 1 radish (large, julienned)
- ✓ 6 spring onions (trimmed and cut into 1-inch pieces)

Time 2–5 days

Makes 2, 500-gm jars

How

- Quarter the cabbage lengthwise through the stem and remove the cores. Cut each quarter into 2-inch-wide strips. Place the cabbage in a large bowl and sprinkle with the salt. Massage the salt into the cabbage until it begins to soften.
- Add water to submerge the cabbage and cover with a bowl. Weigh the plate down with something heavy and let it stand for 1-2 hours. Rinse the cabbage under cold water 3-4 times and let drain in a colander for 20-25 minutes.
- Make the spice paste by mixing grated garlic and ginger, sugar, fish sauce (or water) into a smooth paste. Tip in the chilli flakes (1 tablespoon for mild; increase quantity to suit taste).
- Squeeze out any remaining water from the cabbage and mix in the spice paste. Add the radish and spring onions, and work the paste into the vegetables thoroughly with your hands.
- Transfer the kimchi into a large glass jar and pack down on it (you can place a squeaky-clean glass jar filled with water to weigh the veggies down) until the brine rises and covers the vegetables, leaving at least 1 inch of space at the top. Seal the jar.
- Let sit for 1 to 5 days for the magic of fermentation to happen. The jar must be stored at cool room temperature, out of direct sunlight. Bubbles may rise inside the jar and brine may seep out.
- Check the kimchi once a day. Open the jar and press down on the vegetables with a clean finger or spoon to release gases produced during fermentation. Do a taste test every day and move the jar to a refrigerator when it tastes ripe enough. Refrigerate for up to 3 months.

PRESSURE COOKING

The pressure cooker may have been invented in the 17th century by French-born physicist Denis Papin, but its life has been intertwined with India ever since. No Indian home can do without this cooking staple, which uses water to pressure-cook under high steam. Do you know how to pressure-cook just right, though? We tell you how many whistles are needed to cook one cup of lentils and grains just right.

- Rice: 1-2 whistles
- Dalia: 1-2 whistles
- Potatoes: 2-4 whistles
- Corn: 2-4 whistles
- Yellow moong dal: 3-4 whistles
- Arhar dal: 4-5 whistles
- Split dals (urad, masoor): 3-4 whistles
- Whole dals (masoor, urad, moong, lobia): 4-5 whistles
- Chana: 5-6 whistles
- Chhole: 7-8 whistles
- Rajma: 7-8 whistles

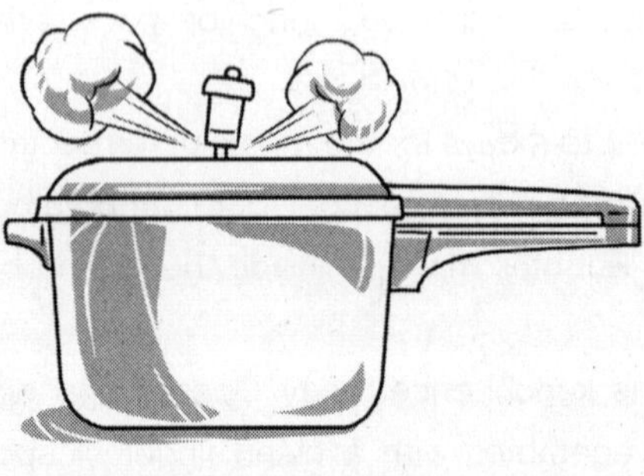

37.

REUSE SPARE ROTIS

Repurposing leftovers and food scraps is safe and can put delicious meals on the table. It can also cut down on food waste and slash your grocery shopping list significantly over time.

How

- **Dahiwali roti:** To a tempering of oil, asafoetida, and mustard seeds, add shredded pieces of roti. Cook for a while, add a glass of buttermilk and let it seep into the pieces. Serve hot.
- **Roti upma:** Grind roti into fine powder. Sauté chopped onions, tomatoes and green chillies. Toss in a few peanuts, turmeric powder, and stir. Mix well and serve.
- **Chapati noodles:** Cut the rotis into thin strips. Stir fry with julienned onions, bell peppers, carrots, and other veggies. Add a dash of soya sauce, and salt and pepper.
- **Roti oats:** Shred the rotis into really small pieces. Boil a cup of milk, tip in the roti shreds, and add your choice of dried fruit and nuts. Cook for 2-3 minutes. Sweeten with honey.
- **Churma ladoos:** Grind roti and jaggery into a coarse mixture. Transfer to a bowl and add ghee to bind. Toss in chopped almonds, pistas and cardamom powder. Shape into roundels.

38.

REPURPOSE LEFTOVER RICE

You can never have too much boiled rice in the fridge. Mixing and mashing it up with different ingredients means a new meal every night.

How

- **Fried rice:** Plain boiled rice can set you up for many one-plate meals. Lemon rice, curd rice, tamarind rice, corn-spinach rice, egg fried rice, chicken fried rice ... You can go on and on.
- **Kheer:** Convert a bowl of leftover rice into a dessert. Boil with milk, and crush lightly. Add dried fruits and nuts, cardamom powder, and a touch of saffron. Simmer till milk is halved.
- **Buddha bowl:** Rice topped with veggies, beans, sprouts, nuts, and drizzled with a dressing is the easiest – and most Instagrammable – way to use up leftovers.
- **Rice fritters:** Mash leftover rice well and mix in a few tablespoons of besan. Add minced veggies of your choice, mix turmeric and chilli powder, and shallow fry on a non-stick pan.
- **Khichdi pakodas:** Spice up leftover khichdi by mixing in besan, mixed veggies, chopped coriander, and amchur powder, and deep-fry roundels in hot oil.

COOK JUST RIGHT

Cooking may be an art, but it's also a science – especially when it comes to cooking times. The food must be just right – neither too hard, nor too soft. Kind of like 'al dente' pasta, which has some chew but isn't overly mushy or tough. All food items need to be cooked for different times, and this table makes it easy to cook a bowlful.

- Noodles: 8-10 minutes
- Elbow macaroni: 8-10 minutes
- Fresh pasta: 2-3 minutes
- Penne: 9-13 minutes
- Farfalle: 13-15 minutes
- Conchiglie: 12-15 minutes
- Fusilli: 11-13 minutes
- Fettuccine: 11-13 minutes
- Lasagna: 12-15 minutes
- Spaghetti: 10-12 minutes
- Vermicelli: 5-7 minutes
- Oatmeal: 5-6 minutes
- Runny-yolk egg: 5 minutes
- Soft-boiled egg: 6 minutes
- Hard-boiled egg: 10 minutes
- Roast chicken: 45 minutes per kg
- Baked potato wedges: 45 minutes
- Basic cookie baking: 8-10 minutes
- Cake: 25-45 minutes
- Quinoa: 20 minutes
- Rice: 15-25 minutes
- Brown rice: 45 minutes

**Do the taste test to ensure preferred 'done'ness*

39.

REUSE OLD BREAD

In most homes, stale bread = French toast. But there's a lot more that can be done with this household staple that lends itself well to a variety of recipes. Butter your bread and get started.

How

- **Jaffle sandwiches:** Almost everything becomes a meal when stuffed between two slices of bread and toasted in a jaffle maker. Leftover veggies, beans, salad, meat, eggs, paneer, hummus, even rice and noodles. Top with a cheese slice and enjoy!
- **Bread upma:** Revive stale bread by crumbling the slices and tossing it in a tempering of oil, asafoetida, mustard seeds, and curry leaves. You can even mix in sautéed onion. Garnish with fresh coriander and serve hot.
- **Breadcrumbs:** Stale slices of bread can be toasted till brown and run through the mixer for homemade breadcrumbs that you can use in numerous recipes. Add a dash of salt.

- **Crouton salad:** A leftover French loaf (and even regular bread) can make your bowl of salad much more filling. Break into cubes, toss in olive oil and herbs, and add to the salad.
- **Bread-and-butter pudding:** Make simple bread-and-butter sandwiches and line a baking dish with them. Mix 2-3 eggs, sugar to taste, a few splashes of milk, vanilla extract, and a teaspoon of cinnamon powder. Pour over the sandwiches and bake at 175°C for 30-35 minutes. Serve with honey or vanilla ice cream.
- **Savoury bread pudding:** Tear bread into small pieces and place in a baking dish. Add a few chopped mushrooms and bell peppers. Mix 2-3 eggs with salt, pepper, and other spices, and pour over the bread-veg mix. Bake at 175°C for 30-35 minutes. Serve with mustard.

40.

REVAMP LEFTOVERS

It doesn't matter what kind of leftovers you have resting in the refrigerator. Almost everything can be repurposed and made into a brand new dish.

How

- **Samosa chaat:** Uneaten samosas/pakodas can be repurposed into a dahi chaat with the addition of sev and chutneys. Or else, tear them into pieces, and toss with sautéed onions, tomatoes and rice for an Indian 'dumpling meal'.
- **Rajma enchiladas:** There are more roles that a bowl of leftover rajma can play other than being the accompaniment to fluffy white rice. It translates into yummy enchiladas when combined with leftover/fresh rotis/tortillas, cheese, and veggies.
- **Rajma chili:** A bowlful of rajma could be a hearty next-day meal when combined with veggies such as carrot, bell peppers, squash, sweet potato, and tomatoes. Throw in ground meat/other beans and add chilli spice.
- **Coleslaw:** This is a good way to use up leftover carrots, beetroot, cabbage, and radish. Use the thick side of the grater

to grate the veggies. Add sprouts if handy, and combine with a dressing of mayonnaise, lemon juice, and a dash of mustard.

- **Fruit-and-nut couscous:** Fridge stuffed with small packs of dried fruit and nuts after a festival? Chop into small pieces and add to cooked couscous/dalia with fresh herbs and lemon juice. Perfect side to grilled chicken or boiled egg salad.
- **Jam cocktail:** The easiest way to repurpose the last bit of jam or marmalade is to make it into a cocktail. Add a shot of vodka/gin to the jar and shake well to combine. Add Cointreau, the juice of a lemon, a sprig of mint, and top off with juice. Salut!
- **Fromage fort:** Give leftover bits of cheeses a glam makeover. Blend them with garlic, a dash of wine, and herbs to make your own Fromage fort ('strong cheese'). Works well as an appetiser or an entrée.
- **Pasta frittatas:** Mix a cup of leftover spaghetti with tofu/paneer, chopped veggies and spices to shallow-fry yummy cutlets or frittatas. The recipe can be replicated with any kind of pasta preparation, and results in a yummy, any-time snack.
- **Leftover pasta soup:** Boil diced veggies in water/stock, and season with salt, pepper, oregano, and herbs. Tip in a few spoonfuls of pasta for a satiating one-pot meal.
- **Pasta cheese balls:** Mash leftover pasta. Mix in a generous amount of cheese and add chopped coriander. Bind with a spoonful of besan/cornflour and deep fry in hot oil.
- **Pizza frittata** Got a couple of slices of leftover pizza? Cut them into small pieces, toss in a few chopped veggies, and mix into beaten eggs. Add your fav spice mix, and set it loose on a pan.

41.

HOW TO PURIFY WATER

Living without the elixir of life is unimaginable. Your fancy-shmancy RO filter may be of no use at all if the taps aren't spouting water. And what if the shops are closed and you can't buy a big batch of packaged water? Making tap water potable will be mandatory – for no human can survive for more than three days without water.

What you need **Time > 45 minutes**

✓ Household bleach
✓ Tincture of iodine
✓ Water disinfection tablets

How

- Boiling is the easiest way to purify any water, and it helps kill pathogenic bacteria, viruses, and protozoa. Filter the water through a clean cloth if it appears cloudy. Bring water to a rolling boil and let it bubble for about 3-5 minutes. Increase the time to about 7 minutes if you live at altitudes above 5,000 feet. Let cool and store in clean containers. Adding a pinch of salt for every litre could get rid of the flat taste that boiled water acquires.

- Household bleach – only the regular, unscented chlorine bleach products – can help disinfect water. Never use perfumed or colour-safe products. Most household bleaches have 6 or 8.25 per cent of sodium hypochlorite. Add 2 drops of bleach for each litre of water. Stir and let sit for 30 minutes. The water will acquire the odour of chlorine. If not, repeat and let sit for 15 more minutes before using.
- Tincture of iodine is commonly available in pharmacies and is often part of first-aid kits. Add 5 drops of 2 per cent tincture of iodine to every 1 litre of water that you want to purify. Add 10 drops if the water is cloudy or coloured. Stir well and let it sit for at least 30 minutes before use. The taste may not be great, but iodine disinfects well.
- Water disinfection tablets typically contain chlorine, iodine, chlorine dioxide, or other disinfecting agents. Available online or in pharmacies, these tablets must be used according to the instructions provided. It's a good idea to store a few packets in your first-aid kit in case of any natural emergencies.

42.

GROW AN HERB GARDEN

Pasta cooking on the stovetop, a glass of vino in your hand, and music playing in the background. What if you could just reach out and pluck some herbs to add a burst of fresh flavour to the penne? Or, pluck fresh lemongrass to add your morning cuppa? It's doable if you grow herbs in small pots – in your verandah or on the window sill. All you need is a warm, sunny place and some pots.

What you need **Time < 2 weeks**

✓ Small pots

✓ Potting mix

✓ Herb saplings

How

- Several herbs are easy to grow, but zero in on the ones you use most. Try rosemary, thyme, mint, chives, lemongrass, coriander, rosemary, and basil. Start with healthy saplings.
- Use individual pots per herb or place separate containers inside large planters. These pots should have drains/holes to

ensure that the roots don't rot. Choose a potting mix which is lighter and more porous than regular soil, and set it in your pots.

- Transfer your saplings into the pots and place in a south-facing direction to help them grow well. Most herbs need about 6 hours of sunlight each day; rotate the pots every week so both sides of the plant receive sun.
- Allow the soil to dry slightly before watering the herbs. Overwatering can kill, so check the moisture level by putting your finger into one inch of soil. Water only if it feels dry. Fertilize with homemade compost (See Hack 96) or chemical-free fertilizer every two weeks.
- Once the plant grows, it's time to harvest your herbs. Cut off the top 2-3 inches of each sprig, but don't cut the plant too close. This will ensure that it keeps growing. Also, never remove more than a third of the plant at a time.

43.

GROW MICROGREENS

Microgreens started gaining popularity about 20 years ago, and continue to be the last word in garnishes and salads. Nothing but the first true leaves – about 2-3 inches tall – of vegetables and herbs, they contain higher levels of vitamins and carotenoids than their mature versions. Try growing your own microgreens using radishes, carrots, spinach, basil, wheat, amaranth, fenugreek, turnips, beetroots, and more.

What you need **Time** < **2 weeks**

- ✓ Pots
- ✓ Potting mix
- ✓ Microgreen seeds

How

- Take your pick of microgreen seeds, instead of sowing mature vegetable seeds. To grow fenugreek and wheatgrass, you can use the seeds. Prep the containers – large, wide trays or baking dishes about 3-5 inches deep work well – with potting soil and sprinkle the seeds in. Cover the seeds with a very thin layer of soil and gently pat the surface.

- Microgreens need sunlight for at least 3-4 hours a day. Put your trays on a windowsill or on a verandah parapet to ensure that the seeds get the sunshine that they need to grow.
- It is necessary that the soil stays moist all the time to ensure proper growth. However, that does not mean wet; that will only clog up the soil. Instead, use a water spray to sprinkle water in batches.
- Sprinkle a little water over the growing greens, twice a day. In 3-4 days, you will observe small leaves growing over the soil with little shoots at the bottom.
- Harvest the microgreens by cutting over the roots – but not too close to the soil – with a sharp pair of scissors. Wash under running water and use in salads, smoothies, sandwiches, and more.

44.

DISHWASH POWDER

A store-bought dishwashing soap is all well and good till your steel wool gets gunk and food particles trapped in it. Avoid this and get a shine on your dishes by using a homemade dishwashing powder. All you need are three easily available ingredients.

What you need **Time** < 10 minutes

✓ 1 cup borax

✓ 1 cup washing soda

✓ 1 cup salt

How

- Mix all the ingredients in a large bowl and mix well. Store in an airtight container.
- Scoop out a spoonful or two into a small saucer when you want to wash dishes, add the juice of a lemon, and get started with the scrubbing.
- The dry ingredients help clean soiled dishes, while the lemon cuts through grease and lends a clean fragrance. This multipurpose cleansing powder can also be used to scrub kitchen counters and balcony areas clean.

MONEY-SAVING TIPS

- **Reduce grocery shopping:** It's a fact well known but not universally acknowledged that the more often you visit a grocery store, the more money you will spend. Try to shop, online or offline, only once a week to see substantial savings in your grocery bills.
- **Buy in bulk:** It makes sense to buy certain items, including many staples, in bulk as they are way cheaper. Stock up on items that you use regularly,
- **Plan your menus:** Planning weekly meals is the best way to make sure you're eating a balanced diet and meeting your nutritional needs. It also lets you optimize your pantry, use leftovers, and makes grocery shopping more efficient.
- **Keep fridge inventories:** Stocking up and freezing food won't do you much good if you don't run regular checks. Check before menu planning, to ensure that nothing stays out of sight till it spoils!
- **Buy seasonal produce:** In-season produce is fresher, cheaper, and has higher nutritional value. Apart from supporting the local economy, it helps reduce food miles and is good for the environment.
- **Start a small garden:** These days, almost everyone can grow vegetables in their balconies; there's no reason not to! Almost anyone can grown a herb garden (See Hack 42).
- **Go meatless:** You may enjoy your non-veg, but that's no reason to eat meat every day. Meat is often the most expensive ingredient, so earmarking some days as meat-free will reduce your grocery bill.
- **Make your own condiments:** All those sauces, dressings, and marinades that you pick up over time add massively to your costs. It's healthier – and way cheaper – to whip up your own salad dressing, salsa, or pesto as and when you need them.
- **Keep a green kitchen:** Ditch paper towels and make your own unsponges (See Hack 88) to quell spills and clean up, put together vinegar-based all-purpose cleaners (See Hack 90), reuse glass jars for storage, have a leftovers day, and freeze all that you can.
- **Plan potluck parties:** The potluck is said to have come into its own in the 1930s during the Great Depression. Today, scheduling a weekly or monthly potluck can be an easy way to hang out with friends/ family, save money on food, and cut entertaining costs.

45.

DIY KITCHEN SPRAY

The kitchen is a hotbed of messes that you need to clean every few hours. This natural cleaning spray can leave your kitchen sparkling.

What you need

✓ 1 cup white vinegar

✓ 1 cup water

✓ 3-4 drops lemon essential oil

✓ 3-5 dried lemon/orange peels (optional)

Time < 5 minutes

Makes 500 ml

How

- Pour in the vinegar and water into a spray bottle. Add the essential oil and citrus peel. Let sit for a couple of days and then remove the peels.
- Spray directly on to kitchen counters or surfaces, or on to a kitchen towel, and wipe area clean. The essential oil tends to gather on top of the bottle, so shake vigorously before each use.
- Don't use on marble countertops and delicate surfaces; instead, try a gentler cleaner of dish soap mixed with hot water.

BONUS HACK

FRUIT & VEGGIE SPRAY

Forget all about store-bought, chemical-laden produce sprays. Make your own natural spray that combines the disinfecting power of vinegar and lemon, and works well with any fruit or vegetable that has a skin or peel. Apples, cucumbers, peppers, tomatoes, grapes ... bring them all on!

What you need **Time < 0.5 hour**

- ✓ 2 cups water
- ✓ 3 tbsp white vinegar
- ✓ 2 tbsp lemon juice
- ✓ Spray bottle

How

- Pour all the ingredients into a large spray bottle and mix.
- Spray on fruits and vegetables, and let sit for a few minutes.
- Scrub if the skin is really dirty; rinse well before consuming.

46.

DEEP CLEAN GAS BURNERS

The collateral damage of making *baingan ka bharta*? Soiled gas burners. Apart from this, the residue and debris that collect over time can clog the burners and reduce the strength of the flame. Clean burners at least once a month to keep your gas in prime condition.

What you need **Time** < 45 minutes

✓ Dish soap
✓ Non-abrasive scrub pad
✓ Old toothbrush
✓ Baking soda
✓ Bobby pin

How

- Shut off the gas valve. Some stoves have a removable ceramic disc on top of the burner to diffuse flames. Lift the discs off and remove the burner heads. Soak in a mix of liquid dish soap and warm water, and let sit for about 30 minutes to loosen hardened gunk.

- Use a non-abrasive scrub pad and an old toothbrush to clean all surfaces of the burner heads and caps. Dig out adamant debris from the holes with a straightened bobby pin. Never use a toothpick; it may break and block the burner heads. Use a paste of baking soda and water to remove the most obstinate stains. Never use bleach or steel wool.
- Wash all parts thoroughly under running water and dry off with a cloth. Allow them to air-dry completely before putting the burners back on to the stove. Clean all the other parts of the stove, scrubbing with a liquid dish soap or a baking soda-water paste, and watch it shine.

47.

CLEAR A BLOCKED SINK

Who hasn't soundly cursed themselves and everyone around them when the sink won't drain? Small bits of food, vegetable peels, lentils, or seeds can block up the drain pipe, and create an incubating ground for bacteria. Take off that apron and clear up the clog to continue with your kitchen chores.

What you need **Time** > 1 hour

✓ 1 cup baking soda

✓ 1 cup white vinegar

✓ Cup plunger/wet-dry vacuum/auger

How

- Fill a large saucepan with water and bring to a rolling boil. Carefully pour directly into the drain in a steady stream. The sink should begin to unclog. If not, wait till the water in the sink cools and repeat. This process is not advisable if the drain is attached to PVC pipes.
- A natural drain cleaner will be much gentler on your piping system as compared to chemical drain openers. Pour one cup

of fresh baking soda down the drain, and follow it up with a cup of white vinegar. Cover the drain opening. Pour in a litre of hot water after 15-20 minutes to unclog completely.

- Try the cup plunger for small blockages. This creates a seal over the sink's hole to create the pressure needed to dislodge the clog. Fill the sink with enough water to submerge the head of the plunger and place the cup over the drain opening. Retain the seal, and plunge up and down rapidly. Ensure that the plunger remains under water level, and you lift it only an inch or so on each time.
- You can also work your wet-dry vacuum by setting the vacuum cleaner up for wet use. Place the hose end at the drain entrance and create a tight seal around the end of the hose and the drain. Turn on the vacuum to the highest setting; the pressure created should dislodge the blockage.
- If nothing works, you may need to bring in the auger. Push the plumbing snake into the drain opening until you meet resistance. This may be the clog; it's time to turn the crank on the device till the cable pushes its way into the clog and moves it forward. The change in resistance will tell you that you are done. Retract and flush the drain. Tip: If you don't have an auger, an opened-up wire hanger could also do the trick.

BONUS HACK

HOMEMADE WINE

Give me books (or the telly), French wine, and popcorn, and I'm all set for a fine evening. The pleasure is compounded if the wine is made at home – yes, it's possible and easy! Pour yourself some one evening, and surprise your family and friends on another with this homemade red.

What you need

✓ 1.5 kg black grapes
✓ 1.5 kgs sugar
✓ 15 gms activated dry yeast
✓ 50 gms wholewheat
✓ 2.6 litres water
✓ Ceramic pickle jar

Time > 42 days

Makes 4 bottles, 1-litre each

How

- Boil the water for 5 minutes and let cool to room temperature. Meanwhile, sterilize the ceramic jar by pouring in boiling water and setting aside for 5 minutes.
- Remove the stem of the grapes and wash 3-5 times, so the fruit is rid of all dirt and chemical traces. Set the grapes on a

clean cloth on a wide tray and let dry. Wash the wheat grains a few times and set on a clean cloth to dry.

- Use a wooden smasher to crush the grapes thoroughly. The goal is to rupture each grape, not extract the maximum juice. Plop into the jar, add the cooled water, and mix in the prepared yeast (follow instructions on the packet).
- Add the wheat into the jar along with half the sugar. Mix with a wooden spoon a couple of times. Close the jar, wrapping the opening with plastic wrap to make it airtight. Place in a cool, dark, and dry place.
- For the next 21 days, set a particular time each day to carefully open the jar, and evenly stir the contents with a clean and dry wooden spatula. Close the jar, ensuring it stays airtight.
- On the 22nd day, open the jar and filter out the contents into a clean, sterilized vessel. Squeeze the grape mix over a filter, emptying the jar. Put the filtered contents back into the jar, add the remaining 750 grams sugar and stir. Close the jar and store in a cool, dry, and dark place for another 21 days.
- After the next 21 days, open the jar, taking care not to shake it, and transfer the clear wine on top into sterilized glass bottles. Drain the jar till you reach the sediment layer at the bottom. And there you have it. Bottles of homemade wine. Salut!

SMART KITCHEN TIPS

- Cast iron pans and pots are all the rage these days, but how do you clean them without causing them to rust? Soapy water will strip away the seasoning. Use a salt scrub and rinse with hot water.
- Get rid of limescale build-up from French presses and other metal kitchen tools, and make them gleam like new by scrubbing them with a solution of 1-part vinegar to 1-part water.
- Pour a cup of white vinegar into the electric kettle and let heat up. This will loosen the most stubborn of scales. Wash thoroughly.
- Rub stained plastic chopping boards with half a lemon on either side, sprinkle salt over, and leave overnight. Scrub for a deep clean.
- Apart from the lemon-and-salt cleaning, oil wooden chopping boards lightly once every week to preserve the wood.
- If you use the mixer attachment often, blend a few tablespoons of salt in it once a month to keep the blades sharp.
- Zap a wet sponge in the microwave for 30 seconds to 1 minute to remove all bacteria.
- Refrigerate rolled-out puris for 10 minutes so they absorb less oil while frying.
- Add a squeeze of lemon juice to your rice while boiling in to make it whiter. Add a dollop of ghee to make sure it doesn't stick and is oh-so-fragrant.
- Store washed and dried lemons in an airtight container to make them last longer.
- Blend equal parts of ginger and garlic with vinegar for a paste that will stay in the fridge for up to 4 months.
- Powder a few things and store for anytime usage: peanuts, sugar, almonds, roasted cumin, coriander seeds, etc.
- Make the ice tray your best friend by freezing coffee shots, chocolate, pesto, stock, tomato puree, herb oil, wine, and flowers.
- Herbs and greens like methi and spinach can be easily dried at home, crumbled, and stored in airtight jars for later use. The same goes for herbs such as basil, coriander, and rosemary.

SECTION 3

BEAUTY

'Beauty begins the moment you decide to be yourself.'

—Coco Chanel

The first time I saw Audrey Hepburn was in *Roman Holiday*, that almost-but-not-quite romantic caper that left us all sighing over what could have been. The luminous, sylphlike Hepburn seemed to radiate a beauty I had never seen on-screen. Her outfits and hair went on to launch hundreds of trends; her face may well have launched a thousand ships and more. She made quite an impression on this young child and was my exacting standard of beauty for years on end. The bangs that framed the elfin face, the oversized sunglasses, the flipped-out hair, and the little sleeveless dresses combined to create an elegant Hollywood icon, whose beauty and appeal were timeless.

Interestingly, the actor and humanitarian didn't agree. 'Whenever I hear or read I'm beautiful, I simply don't understand it ... I'm certainly not beautiful in any conventional way,' she is reported to have said in an interview.[1]

Standards of beauty are subjective, and everyone has their own opinions. The idea of beauty differs from person to person, region to region, country to country. However, it is always shifting, and has become more inclusive and wide-ranging in the last decade.

But beauty is more than outward appearances. It's more than how your hair falls, the shape of your eyebrows, the softness of your skin, the flush in your cheeks, and the mystery in your eyes. It's what's inside that makes you beautiful.

Right?

Hepburn herself said it in another interview: 'Makeup can only make you look pretty on the outside, but it doesn't help if you're ugly on the inside. Unless you eat the makeup.'[2]

Erm, that's all well and good to read and hear, but it's a different story when you face the mirror. Beauty on the inside may be far more precious – and unattainable – than beauty on the outside, but we all want the reflection to mirror more of the outside kind.

That's the reason why, as a teenager, I cut off my hair to create wispy bangs (which, honest to god, turned out kinda mousy) and subjected myself to the abject torture of threading every fifteen days, ouching and twisting as the lady told me to stretch the skin by pushing my tongue against the upper lip.

It was why my BFF decided to give her hair a super-extreme makeover with bleach, and lived with an almost orange mane for more than a month. Needless to say, she managed to turn numerous heads, including that of the man she went on to marry!

Like me and her, millions of people across the world make salon appointments, buy beauty products, and seek expert advice in a quest to improve their appearance.

Inner beauty – bright eyes, a radiance within, and all that razzmatazz – is hard to achieve, and most of us tend to think of it as a long-term quest. Outer beauty, on the other hand, is something of a short-term goal and seems doable.

That zit you need to get rid of, those under-eye dark circles that are all you see when you come face to face with yourself in the mirror, or the cracked heels that say things about you that you don't want revealed ... These outwardly problems and many, many more are what the beauty industry aims to solve.

According to a report by Allied Market Research, the global cosmetics industry generated $380.2 billion in 2019, and is expected to reach $463.5 billion by 2027, witnessing a compound annual general rate (CAGR) of 5.3 per cent from 2021 to 2027.[3]

This report, of course, does not account for COVID-19 and the consequent social distancing norms, which forced us to rethink even the 'lipstick index'.[4] The term was coined by Leonard Lauder, the chairman of cosmetics giant Estée Lauder, in the 2001 recession after lipstick sales in America increased by 11 per cent in the autumn of that year. It revealed that economic distress or not, people will spend – but yes, prudently. So big-ticket items such as snazzy cars will stay in showrooms and designer bags will continue to make shop shelves their home as women turn to smaller, affordable indulgences. Hello, *lipsticks*!

But the pandemic forced us to hide our mouths behind masks, and that led to the emergence of a new index. Estee Lauder CEO Fabrizio Freda said the lipstick index had been substituted by the moisturizer index, but the 'concept of the index is still there'. The concept continued to change as we all hunkered down at home, with wellness and well-being occupying the most mindspace.

Around the world, people learnt to satisfy beauty demands and needs on their own – from giving themselves their first haircut and figuring out how to thread facial hair to making their own natural blush and lip balm. I did things I had never done – gave the husband a crew cut, trimmed the daughter's bangs, and relied more on homemade scrubs and masks than I ever had before.

Looking good helps us feel even better, which is why most of us googled DIY beauty products and processes. In today's time, thanks to mobile phones and editing apps that allow better control over photos, beauty often seems to be in the hands, not the eye, of the beholder. But many of those hands – like mine – are choosing to make natural products to feel more beautiful and increase our sense of self-worth!

I find that going down the homemade beauty path is like an adventure. Be it slathering on handmade body lotion after a shower, giving yourself a killer facial massage before hitting the bed, or putting together a luxurious hand soak to return the plumpness to your fingers, it's a feeling like none other. Putting together a fruit-based facial mask and applying edible gunk on to the face may not make me look the most beautiful at that time. But it leaves me with a sense of accomplishment that brings a smile to my lips! And isn't smiling one of the best beauty remedies?

48.

REETHA, AMLA AND SHIKAKAI SHAMPOO

Used by our great-grandmothers and grandmothers to keep their crowning glory in top form, this home remedy does take a while to put together. But the results are well worth it – soft, strong, and shining hair without any chemical-laden shampoos and conditioners.

What you need **Time** < 8 hours

✓ 8-10 shikakai pods
✓ 12-15 reetha pods (soap nuts)
✓ 1 tbsp amla powder
✓ 4 cups water

How

- Pour the water into a large bowl and soak all the ingredients overnight. You can also use the powdered form of shikakai and reetha, if those are handy. Transfer the mixture into a saucepan the next morning, and boil until the pods soften completely (this should take about 30-45 minutes).

- Let cool and then roughly squash the ingredients together by hand. Strain and use to wash your hair. The shikakai nourishes hair follicles, and imparts shine and softness, the reetha cleanses the hair and promote a growth, and the amla reduces hair loss and greying.
- Store the excess in a plastic/glass bottle. This shampoo may not lather as much as store-bought ones, but it helps cleanse the hair just as well. Use twice if needed.

SMART TIPS

- Say bye-bye to clarifying shampoos forever. A tablespoon of baking soda mixed with your regular shampoo helps exfoliate and leaves your scalp feeling squeaky clean.
- Reserve the water used to boil potatoes and use for a final rinse after your hair wash for lustrous waves. Ditto with leftover black tea: squeeze in half a lemon for added shine.

BONUS HACK

DRY SHAMPOO

A dry shampoo can help convert a bad hair day into a good one. But chances are that you need it NOW; there's no time to shop online or run to your favourite store. Here's a quick mix.

What you need **Time** < 5 minutes

✓ 2 tbsps arrowroot powder
✓ 2-3 tbsps unsweetened cocoa powder
✓ 2-3 drops tea tree oil (optional)

How

- Put the arrowroot powder (you can also use cornstarch) and cocoa powder in a bowl, and whisk till combined. Add the essential oil and transfer the powder into an airtight glass jar.
- Use a voluminous makeup brush to apply the powder to your roots, especially around the forehead and temples where the hair tends to fall flat. Apply to the rest of your scalp by flipping your head over.
- Let it sit for about 5 minutes and brush/comb your hair from root to tip to distribute the powder evenly.

49.

MIRACLE HAIR OIL

Hard water, chemical-laced products, endless styling ... With so much abuse, is it any wonder that your hair is giving up? Thinning, coarse, dull strands accompanied by constant hair fall are signs that your hair needs some TLC. This nutrient-rich oil will turn the tide. and make your locks thick and glossy

What you need **Time < 3 days**

- ✓ 500 ml coconut oil
- ✓ 1 onion, chopped
- ✓ 3 garlic cloves
- ✓ 15-20 curry leaves
- ✓ A handful hibiscus flowers and leaves (dried naturally or in the oven)

How

- Sauté the onion and garlic in a spoonful of coconut oil, and then add the rest of oil. Heat till warm. Don't let it bubble or boil.

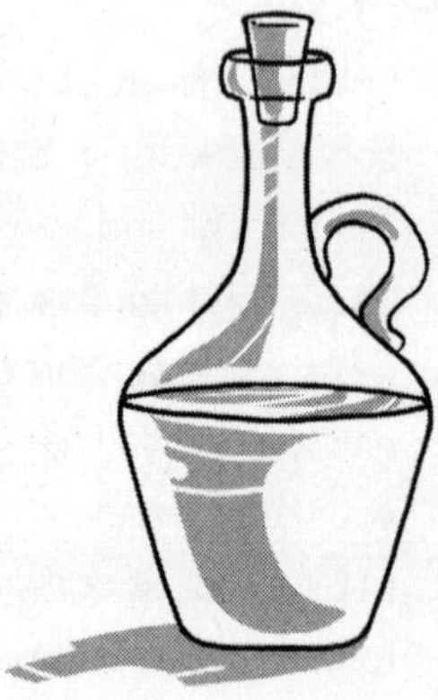

- Toss in the curry leaves and hibiscus. Let the onion and leaves steep in the oil for 2-3 days.
- Strain and store in a cool, dry place. Warm it up a bit before applying.

SMART TIPS

- Apply a mix of apple cider vinegar and water, or lemon juice and coconut oil to rid your hair of dandruff.
- Help your hair colour stand out with a simple apple cider rinse. Add a cup of apple cider to one mug of cold water and pour over washed hair.
- No apple cider vinegar at home? Boil some tea leaves in a saucepan and let cool overnight. Juice a lemon and use as a final rinse.

50.

DEEP CONDITIONING TREATMENT FOR HAIR

Incorporating a deep conditioning treatment into your beauty regimen keeps your hair healthy and hydrated. Whisk this one at home for soft and shiny tresses.

What you need

- ✓ 1 banana (ripe)
- ✓ 1 tbsps fenugreek seeds (soaked overnight)
- ✓ 1 tbsps yoghurt
- ✓ 1 tbsps honey
- ✓ 2 tbsps coconut/olive oil
- ✓ 1 tbsps vitamin E oil
- ✓ 1 lemon (juiced)

Time > 10 minutes

How

- Put all the ingredients in the small jar of your mixer and whizz. The runny paste, which combines oils, fruit, seeds, and honey, will provide your hair with all the moisture and nutrition it needs.
- Leave on hair for an hour and wash off. Use once a week.

BONUS HACK

LUSCIOUS LIP SCRUB

Soft, kissable lips are easy to score if you use a lip scrub once a week. It helps exfoliate and moisturize dry, peeling lips, and keeps them baby soft through every season. Experiment with a variety of ingredients or ready this simple standby for anytime use.

What you need **Time** < 10 minutes

- ✓ 1 tsp sugar
- ✓ 1 tsp honey
- ✓ 2-3 drops lemon juice

How

- Tip the sugar into the honey in a small bowl. Honey is a humectant that locks in moisture while the sugar acts as an exfoliator. You can also replace it with ghee or petroleum jelly.
- Add the lemon juice – a natural depigmentation agent – and mix lightly. Use your fingers to dab on to your lips and gently massage for a couple of minutes.
- Wash off with water or wipe with a wet cotton pad to reveal supple, beautiful lips.

51.

GHEE KAJAL

An Indian girl's makeup arsenal is incomplete without kajal. Be it *soorma*, kajal, or kohl, this black liner endows eyes with beauty and a sense of mystery. Traditionally made in most Indian households with ghee, it also provides a cooling and soothing effect.

What you need **Time** > 2 hours

- ✓ 3 tbsps cow ghee
- ✓ A pinch of organic sandalwood powder (optional)
- ✓ 1 large diya (brass or clay)
- ✓ 2 tall bowls of the same height
- ✓ 1 plate (silver, copper, or steel)

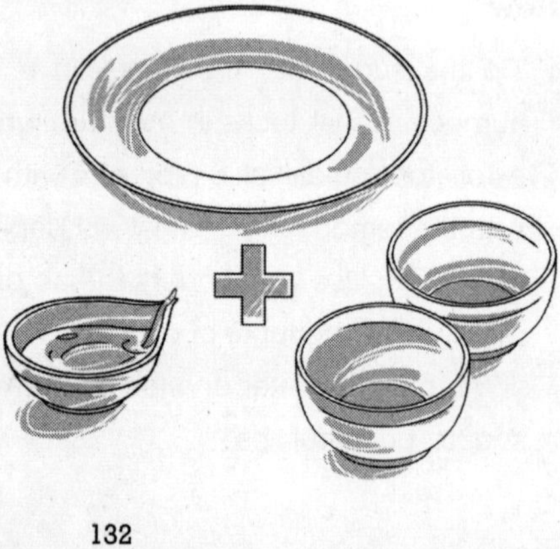

How

- Mix the sandalwood powder into the ghee and fill into the diya. Let the baati soak for a few minutes. Place the diya between the two bowls, light it and then cover the entire thing with a plate. The flame should flicker quite near the bottom of the plate.
- Pour cold water in the plate (this is said to help collect more soot, which makes your kajal that glistening, sooty black) and let the baati die out.
- Lift up the plate with a cloth as it may be hot and flip it over where all the soot would have gathered. Remove with a blunt knife and put into a small glass container. Add a couple of drops of ghee to help it settle into a thickish paste that you can apply with your finger or a brush.

52.

NATURAL EYE SHADOW

Move over, fancy eye shadow palettes from fancier brands! Making your own eye shadow gives you complete control over the ingredients you use, and lets you customize the hue and shade. All you need is a base – arrowroot powder is perfect, but you can replace it with cornstarch or cream of tartar – and other natural ingredients to add colour to your eyes!

What you need **Time** < 30 minutes

✓ 6 tsps arrowroot powder

✓ Cocoa powder (brown), beetroot powder (pink), spirulina/basil (green), activated charcoal (black/grey), nutmeg (golden brown), turmeric (golden yellow), as per colour desired

How

- Mix the coloured, natural ingredients with a teaspoon each of arrowroot powder to create a powder eye shadow of your choice. You can experiment with the quantities to create lighter/darker shades.
- Store in small jars for up to 3 months.

SMART TIPS

- Add a dollop of shea butter to the homemade mixture to make a cream eye shadow. This will moisturize your eyelids, prevent the colour from bleeding, and give your eyes a shiny highlight.
- Dust an eyeshadow (in the same colour family as your hair) along your hair parting. Shading your scalp slightly makes your hair look fuller.
- Add a tint to your brows and keep them in place by dabbing them lightly with a mix of eyeshadow powder (two times lighter than your natural hair colour) and aloe vera gel.
- Mix a tablespoon of arrowroot powder with a tablespoon of beetroot powder (or more or less till you like the colour), to create a natural blush. A 1:1 ratio leads to a lighter hue, while a 2:1 (beetroot:arrowroot) creates a darker pink. Experiment by adding pinches of turmeric to get a peachy blush and cocoa to darken the pink.

53.

THREAD YOUR UPPER LIP

Aunt Marge may have been as happily hirsute as Uncle Vernon (remember your Harry Potter?), but not many of us would want to make a style statement like that. A thread, mirror, and pliable fingers are all you need to pluck out all the hair you don't want to see!

What you need **Time** < 20 minutes

✓ Thread

✓ A pinch of talcum powder

✓ Mirror

How

- Cut the thread to 30 cm length and tie the ends together to form a large loop. Keep your palms facing inwards and loop the string over the outside of your fingers and stretch outward to form a rectangle – the way you do when making string figures in cat's cradle.

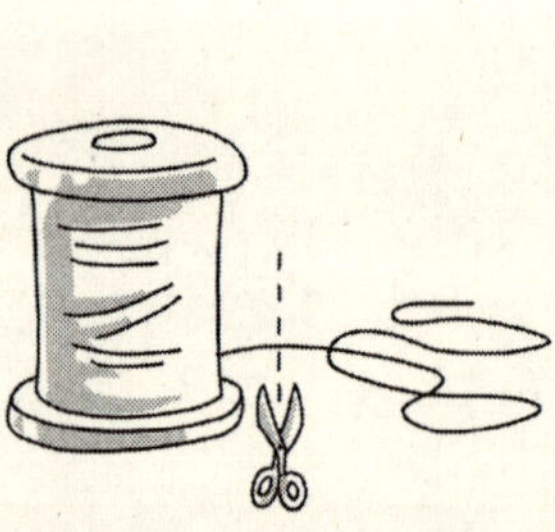

- Move both hands in opposing circular movements 10 times. This will form a twisted line along the centre of the loop. Release your little and forefingers, so only the thumbs, middle fingers, and ring fingers are inside the string loop. Pull the string taut and alternate lifting the middle finger on each hand. This will move the twisted section from side to side and works to catch and pluck out hair.

- Powder your upper lip. Press your lips together or place your tongue under specific sections of your upper lip to make the area taut. Hold the string and move the twists in the thread to the right by lifting your left middle finger.

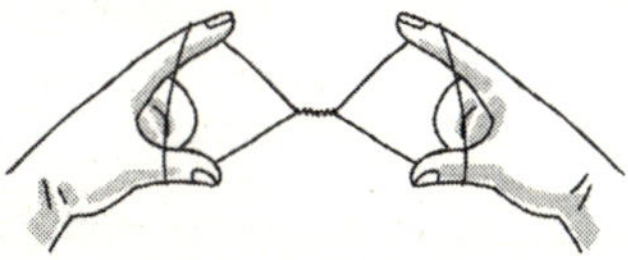

- Place the twisted section to the outside right of your lips. Keep the string in contact with your skin, and lift the right middle finger to move the twist along the thread and catch any hairs. Repeat on the other side.

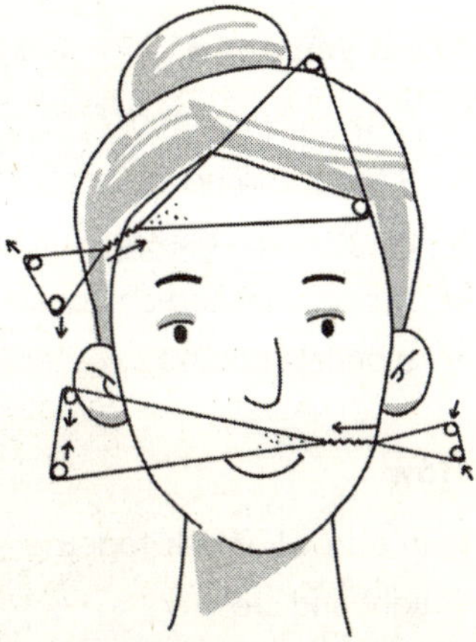

- Once you're a pro at threading your upper lip, you can slowly try threading your forehead and – ultimately – ace the brow game.

54.

NATURAL TOOTHPASTE

The most effective wake-up call in the morning is having the toothbrush hit your teeth. But what happens if you run out of toothpaste? A good toothpaste comprises abrasives, active ingredients, and flavourings – and *tooth be told*, it's possible to do this the homemade way.

What you need **Time < 15 minutes**

✓ 8 tbsps coconut oil

✓ 8 tbsps baking soda

✓ 25-30 drops essential oil (clove, eucalyptus or peppermint)

✓ 1 tbsp activated charcoal (optional)

✓ 8 pellets natural sweetener (optional), or 2 tsps salt

How

- In a bowl, whisk together all the ingredients till the blend is light and creamy.
- Store in a small glass jar and either refrigerate (this helps it solidify) or keep at room temperature (this gives you a runny toothpaste). Use the back of a spoon to spread it on to your toothbrush. Keep outside for 2-3 weeks and refrigerated for up to 5 weeks.

55.

EASY MOUTHWASH

Who hasn't reached out for a bottle of mouthwash and swilled it around to get rid of bad breath or just to feel clean? Store-bought mouthwashes claim to help fight cavities and plaque, but a homemade recipe can also keep your breath at its best.

What you need **Time** < 5 minutes

- ✓ 25 ml filtered water
- ✓ 1 tbsp salt
- ✓ 1 tbsp baking soda
- ✓ 2-3 drops essential oil (clove/peppermint)

How

- Pour the water into a glass bottle.
- Add the salt, soda, and essential oil, and shake well till they dissolve. The salt reduces inflammation by contracting tissues and neutralizes bacteria, while the baking soda, which has a pH of around 9, helps alkalize the mouth. Balancing your oral pH can keep your teeth and gums in pristine condition.

56.

KILLER FACIAL MASSAGE

A facial massage can help release tension in the jaw and scalp, improve blood circulation, aid in the flow of lymphatic fluid, and smoothen fine lines. Done regularly (and correctly), it will give your face a natural glow and you'll no longer need to spend thousands at the salon every month.

What you need **Time** < 30 minutes

✓ Oil, serum, or cream, of your choice

How

- Wet your hands with the oil/serum/cream. Place all 10 fingertips above your eyebrows. Slowly push them up to the top of your forehead and into your scalp, with mild pressure. Repeat 5-8 times.
- Gently pinch your eyebrows from the inner edge, using the thumb and index finger. Pinch 4-5 times as you move to the outer edge. Repeat the movement 5 times.
- Place the tips of your index and middle fingers on your temples. Slowly massage for a few seconds before gliding your fingers under the eye area, to the bridge of your nose, and then up and

over your eyebrows. End at your temple without losing contact (kind of like making a figure of 8). Repeat 5-8 times.

- Slide your fingertips from your temples and down the sides of your face towards your neck. Repeat 4-5 times.
- Make a V with your index and middle fingers. Place your index finger just above your upper lip and your middle finger just below your bottom lip. Gently pull both fingers towards your ear simultaneously. Repeat 5-8 times.
- Place both hands, palms down, on your chest. Slowly glide the left hand up your chest and neck, towards the chin. Do this 5-8 times. Repeat with the right hand.
- Use your fingertips to work your way through your scalp, The scalp can take more pressure, so rub hard to loosen the tightness.
- Close your eyes and place both hands over your face gently. Take a few deep, relaxing breaths. Open your eyes after 10 such rounds to see a brighter world!

HOMEMADE SERUMS

FOR BRIGHTER SKIN	FOR OILY SKIN	FOR DRY SKIN
1 tbsp yoghurt + few drops of lemon juice	1 tbsp aloe vera gel + a pinch of turmeric	1 tbsp aloe vera gel + 1 tsp rose water
1 tbsp raw milk + ½ tbsp tomato juice	1 tbsp honey + few drops of lemon juice	1 tbsp yoghurt + ½ tbsp honey
1 tbsp aloe vera gel + ½ tbsp papaya paste	1 tbsp cucumber juice + ½ tbsp aloe vera gel	1 tbsp coconut oil + ½ tbsp aloe vera gel

BONUS HACK

DIY SHEET MASK

Koreans – sticklers for dewy, glass-like skin – are said to have given the sheet mask to the world, and now, almost every beauty company offers its own versions and variants. But there's no need to make weekly spends on this skincare essential, given that it's so easy to do at home.

What you need **Time < 15 minutes**

✓ Cotton handkerchief

✓ Liquids to make homemade serums

How

- A recyclable sheet mask can last you months. Cut a cotton hanky to the size of your face and cut out holes for your eyes, mouth, and nose. Stitch the edges to keep them from unravelling.
- A DIY sheet mask can easily be customized to your skin type, courtesy the experimentation you can do with liquid ingredient combinations. Whip up your own serum (consult table above).
- Prepare the liquid you intend to use in a bowl. Add filtered water if you need to make it thinner. Dip your mask into the

liquid and let it soak for 5-10 minutes. Bring (don't wring) out the mask, and let the extra liquid slide back into the bowl.

- Unfold the DIY sheet mask and gently lay it on your face, aligning the holes with your eyes, nose, and mouth. Smooth out wrinkles and add more homemade serum if the mask seems dry. Leave on your face for 20-25 minutes.

One-Tablespoon Face Packs

Every skin type is unique, but these combinations work for almost everyone. Experiment with the quantity, but rule of thumb: a tablespoon of each. Those with normal skin are lucky; they can try both! Make a smooth paste and apply.

FOR DRY SKIN	FOR OILY SKIN
Malai + honey	Yoghurt + a pinch of turmeric
Banana + yoghurt	Glycerine + lemon juice
Papaya + raw milk	Multani mitti + cucumber juice
Egg yolk + honey	Gram flour + tomato juice
Aloe vera + honey	Papaya + honey
Rice flour + aloe vera	Egg white + honey
Almond paste + yoghurt	Honey + lemon

57.

MOISTURIZING FACE MIST

During the hot Indian summer, all we want is some thing cooling and refreshing for our skin. This facial mist does all that – and also moisturizes. Make a big batch and use through the summer!

What you need

Time < 10 minutes

- ✓ 2 cups distilled water
- ✓ 1 tbsp aloe vera gel
- ✓ 1 tbsp glycerine
- ✓ 3-5 drops rose essential oil
- ✓ 2 tbsps rose water
- ✓ 1 vitamin E capsule

How

- Pour the water into a glass bowl and add the other ingredients. Puncture the capsule, and drain the oil into the mix.
- Whisk thoroughly and fill into a spray bottle. Screw the bottle shut and store in the refrigerator for best results.
- Give it a good shake every time you want to spray your face.

58.

AU NATUREL DEO

You're at a meeting, that first date, or just hanging with friends over the weekend when that familiar smell of BO assails you. This all-natural deodorant will keep you smelling and feeling great. Also, it may be the cheapest deo you ever used!

What you need **Time** < 10 minutes

- ✓ ¼ cup coconut oil
- ✓ ¼ cup arrowroot powder
- ✓ ¼ cup baking soda
- ✓ 8-10 drops essential oil (orange, lavender, tea tree, etc.)

How

- Pour melted coconut oil into a small glass jar. Mix in an essential oil of your choice.
- Add the arrowroot powder and baking soda, and mix thoroughly. Store in the refrigerator: it will last you months.
- To use, scoop out with a small spoon and apply on your armpits with your fingers.

59.

SUGAR WAX

Centuries ago, the Romans got rid of unwanted body hair with makeshift razors. In Cleopatra's time, sugaring was the primary method of hair removal. It may be compared to modern waxing methods, but sugaring is different: the ingredients come out of your kitchen and no cloth strips are used. And it leaves you with much softer, smoother skin!

What you need **Time < 1 hour**

✓ 1 cup white sugar
✓ 2 tbsps lemon juice
✓ 2 tbsps warm water

How

- Put all the ingredients in a medium-sized saucepan and place on the stove. Bring to a boil over high heat, stirring frequently to avoid burning. Reduce to medium heat once the mixture starts bubbling, and continue to stir.
- Turn the heat off when the mixture turns golden brown (this is why white sugar is preferred over brown). At this stage, the

sugar paste should look like syrup, not honey. Transfer to a glass bowl and let cool for 30 minutes. It can be used when warm (not hot) and pliable.

- Wash and dry the area where you want to use the sugar wax. Hold the waxy paste with the tips of your fingers and thumb, and spread over the area – in the direction of hair growth. Use the other hand to pull the skin taut and pull off the strip quickly in the opposite direction in a movement parallel to the skin. Voila!

60.

LUXURIOUS HAND AND FOOT SOAK

Your hands are at work all day – whether you're in the kitchen, out shopping, or furiously pounding away at the laptop. Your feet, meanwhile, are up as long as you are and keep you going. Changing seasons and continued water exposure can be hard on your limbs, and it's a good idea to give them a luxurious soak once in a while.

What you need **Time < 20 mins**

✓ 1 cup milk, 1 cup water (for hands)/
1 glass milk + 2 mugs water (for feet)

✓ 2 tbsps coconut/olive oil

✓ 1 tbsp oatmeal (powdered)

How

- Pour the warmed milk into a deep bowl/bucket. Mix in the powdered oats and oil. For that luxurious spa feel, throw in some rose petals/an essential oil of your choice.

- Place your hands/feet in the bowl/bucket (make good use of the time at hand by slathering on a face mask), and let them soak in this goodness for about 10 minutes.
- Wash the liquid off your hands and feet. Pat dry on a towel and moisturize with a heavy cream to keep your hands and feet as soft as a baby's bum for longer.

SMART TIPS

- Save a piece of the banana you're eating, mash it together with a teaspoon full of sugar, and scrub till the cubes melt for supple hands.
- Take a teaspoon of sugar and a few drops of lemon juice in your palm, and scrub till the mix melts to get rid of spots on your hands.
- Prep a moisturizing hand mask by mixing multani mitti with yoghurt and a few drops of coconut oil. Apply and let dry off.

61.

HOMEMADE LOTION BAR

If even slathering on body lotion seems like too much effort, you're sure to love the idea of a rich moisturizing bar that you can run over your hands, legs, and feet.

What you need

- ✓ 1 cup coconut oil
- ✓ 1 cup beeswax
- ✓ 2-3 drops essential oil (try lavender, rose, or vanilla)

Time < 30 minutes

Makes 5-6 bars

How

- Put the coconut oil and beeswax in a saucepan, and place over low heat. Chip the beeswax to help it melt faster. Add the essential oil and let it cool a bit.
- Pour the mixture into muffin tins or silicon moulds. Place the tray in the refrigerator to help the bars solidify.
- Add pure cocoa or shea butter to the mix (a third of each) to increase the bar's emollient-like qualities. Remove from the moulds and run over your hands to see the transformation. Store in refrigerator to avoid melting.

BONUS HACK

SCRUB-A-DUB-DUB BODY SCRUB

This scrub smells so delicious that you will be forgiven for wanting to polish it off – instead of letting it exfoliate and polish your body. The spicy scents are redolent of baking and Christmas, and are sure to put you in a great mood. Fa-la-la-la-la!

What you need

- ✓ 1 cup sugar (brown or white)
- ✓ 1 cup coconut oil
- ✓ 2 tbsps vitamin E oil (optional)
- ✓ 2 tsps vanilla extract
- ✓ 1 tsps cinnamon powder
- ✓ ½ tsp clove powder
- ✓ ½ tsp ginger powder
- ✓ ½ tsp nutmeg powder

Time < 15 minutes

How

- Tip the sugar into a lidded glass jar and add the coconut oil. The tiny sugar cubes work well as a natural exfoliator.
- Mix in all the other ingredients.
- Store at room temperature for up to 4 months.

BEAUTY HACKS EVERYONE MUST KNOW

- While chopping a tomato, reserve a piece and rub it on your face. The juice brightens your skin.
- A spoonful of yoghurt is the best face mask – for every kind of skin. Add a couple of drops of lemon, a dab of honey, and a dash of turmeric to brighten your skin.
- Toss a couple of green tea bags in the bathtub or your bucket of hot water for a relaxing bath. Reuse these bags by chilling them and applying on tired eyes.
- Never toss away a used lemon half. Quickly rub the juice into your elbows, knees, and ankles to reduce the darkening.
- Apply a layer of egg white on your nose and place a paper napkin strip on it. Repeat with another egg-and-tissue layer when dry. Peel off when completely dry to remove blackheads.
- Apply a smidgen of coconut oil around your eyes and mouth every night to prevent and smoothen out crow's feet and laugh lines.
- Use a piece of tape as a stencil to draw the perfect winged eyeliner even when you're in a hurry.
- Mascara running dry? Add a few drops of your contact lens solution to the bottle to get it back in action.
- Out of nail polish remover? Mix lemon juice and vinegar for a homemade solution or simply apply a coat of nail polish and wipe off.
- Use sanitizer to wipe sunglasses, prescription eyeglasses, and mobile phone regularly to kill bacteria and prevent skin breakouts.

SECTION 4

HEALTH AND WELL-BEING

'The greatest wealth is health.'

—Virgil

Disprin for headaches, paracetamol for any kind of fever, an antacid after a spicy meal. Who hasn't resorted to pill-popping when plagued by everyday maladies? It ain't good for us; yet, we continue doing it.

In a world where everything goes around in circles - be it trends, fashions, habits, and propensities - perhaps it's time to go back to grandma's way of living. Even though we were told she knew best, we never really believed it. But, over the years, plentiful research and studies have showed that grandma *really* did know best. Her focus on natural ways of healing and restoring is what the world is going back to, isn't it? Nothing else accounts for the rise in interest in alternative and complementary therapies worldwide.

The pandemic has spotlighted the fragile state of India's healthcare system, and heightened awareness about the importance of and relationship between immunity, prevention, and health. This could be the reason for the burgeoning interest in Ayurveda, a Sanskrit word that translates into the 'science of life'. There isn't any scientific evidence that Ayurvedic treatments can prevent or help cure the coronavirus, but that didn't stop millions of people from turning to herbs, spices, and natural remedies to try and stay on top of their health.

According to research by iMarc Group, India's Ayurvedic products market reached a value of Rs 515.5 billion in 2021. But we want more of the Ayurveda pie! The report details that the market is likely to reach Rs 1,536.9 billion by 2027, exhibiting a CAGR of 19.78 per cent during 2022-2027.[1]

During the pandemic, I could almost hear my own grandma saying 'I told you so' as I made an immunity-boosting herb-and-spice tea every day without fail. The lady really knew what she was talking about! She was spot on when she persisted in saying that the kitchen wasn't just the heart of the home; it housed all the ingredients that could keep the heart – and more – healthy.

Apart from stocking staples, condiments, and more, kitchen shelves are a cornucopia of health and wellness, courtesy the many herbs, spices, and other ingredients that reside here. Reason enough to tap into this always-available source of health, isn't it? Don't think of it as a magic pill; consider it more like a slow-acting panacea to all-round healthiness.

But today's world needs you to know more than just kitchen cures. It's vital to know life-saving skills, such as how to perform CPR, recognize the signs of a stroke, simple desk exercises to keep you supple, eye exercises to maintain eye health, and – in these times of emotional turbulence – how to prioritize your mental health.

Grandma knew more than a bit about that as well. She was way ahead of her time when it came to looking after her physical and mental health, with little habits that made it easier to do so – short walks (so what if they were in the home?) after every meal, stretching out her joints and muscles, washing her eyes at the beginning and end of each day, and a little bit of exercising on the spot when she could do so.

Meditation and mindfulness may be the buzzwords today, but she had a routine that set aside a few minutes every day to focus on the supreme power. What was that, if not meditation? At that time, honestly, it seemed like too little, not enough. Now, when I think about the compounded benefits of good habits, the mind honestly boggles.

Doing a little bit every single day, she, and millions of grandmums around the world, were living the most important life tenet of all: showing up. Showing up is our ability to remain committed to and consistent in our actions. But, over the last few years, showing up has become workplace related. An article in *Harvard Business Review* states that the first secret of success is showing up, as in 'addition to providing knowledge and relationships, showing up is a sign of caring'.[2]

Actor and comedian Woody Allen once said that 80 per cent of success in life is just showing up. He may have said and done multiple questionable things since then, but this statement continues to ring true. Showing up should begin with you, for your own self. It is vital to do this consistently to maintain and enhance your physical, mental, and emotional health. Health isn't a destination; it's a process – one that involves many facets that must be considered and aligned together.

As Plato rightly said, 'The part can never be well unless the whole is well.'

62. BASIC FIRST AID HACKS

No one knows when a medical emergency may strike. Being prepared and knowing the best course of action will help you deal with the situation. That said, it's vital to remain calm during injuries and emergencies. This will help you provide better first aid – to yourself or someone else – until professional help gets there.

How

- **Remove a splinter:** The safety-pin or needle method to get out a splinter from the skin isn't exactly easy. The simplest hack to get splinters out is to spread a thin layer of craft glue over the affected area. Let dry and peel off. Splinters are most likely to adhere themselves to the glue, making them easier to remove. Once the splinter is out, dab a bit of antiseptic on the wound/prick. If the wound is visibly open, you may put on a Band-Aid as well.
- **Save a knocked-out tooth:** A tooth that's fallen out during a rough game of football can be saved. Place it in a jar of milk and head to the dentist. If that's not possible, simply pop the tooth into a thin piece of gauze and pop into your mouth – that could make all the difference – and run to the dentist. Dab

some turmeric on to a piece of cotton, place at the afflicted spot, and press hard to stop bleeding.

- **Take care of a nosebleed:** Sit upright, leaning forward to decrease pressure and to prevent swallowing blood. Don't blow your nose. Hold your nostrils for 10-15 minutes and breathe through your mouth. Repeat if necessary. Head to the hospital if the bleeding continues.
- **Stop bleeding from a minor wound:** Put direct pressure on the cut with a clean towel or sterile gauze. Rub with ice to help the blood clot faster, if needed. Clean the wound with an antiseptic solution, apply an ointment, and bandage.
- **Stem bleeding from a cut vein/artery:** The loss of blood can be alarming, but stay calm and apply pressure to stem the flow. If it doesn't stop, you may need to fashion a tourniquet. Cut up a shirt lengthwise, fold it, and wrap it 1 to 2 inches above the wound. Tighten until the bleeding stops. Inflating the cuff of a blood-pressure monitor can also work. Head to a hospital immediately because tissues start to die from lack of blood in 4 to 6 hours, increasing the likelihood of loss of a limb.
- **Grow out an ingrown toenail:** Soak your foot in warm water for about 10 minutes. Dry and gently push a thin piece of gauze under the edge of the ingrown toenail to try and raise it. Repeat the soaking every four to six hours and reinsert the gauze if it falls out. Do this until the toenail grows right.
- **Deal with a sprain or bad bruise:** The best way to deal with bruises and sprains is the RICE method. Rest the area. Ice it for about 10 minutes, with a cloth placed between your skin and the ice pack. Compress the area with an elastic bandage.

Elevate the injury above heart level. Splint the injury so you don't move and aggravate it.

- **Treat burns and scalds:** Burns are usually caused by dry heat, while scalding is the effect of moist heat, such as boiling water, steam, hot oil or tar. The area tends to become sterile, and it is best to try and keep it that way. Avoid handling the affected area, do not remove clothing, and do not apply lotions/creams or break the blisters. Cover the area with a dry sterile dressing or clean and washed linen, and head to the doctor.
- **Deal with dog and cat bites:** These bites are usually small wounds; wash with water to remove bacteria-filled saliva. Cover with a clean, dry dressing. See a doctor if the bite is caused by an unknown dog (one who's not vaccinated), doesn't stop bleeding, has gone to the bone or tendons, or causes intense pain/nausea.
- **Handle a seizure:** The most common cause of seizures is epilepsy and the symptoms are many: unconsciousness, muscle contractions/convulsions, weakness, loss of sensation, clouded awareness, fidgeting, confusion, and sleepiness. Keep the person safe until the seizure is over – loosen their clothing and set aside all nearby hard/sharp objects. Don't hold the person down or try to curb movements; place them on the side to keep airway clear. Time the length of the seizure and report to the doctor.
- **Help someone who is choking:** Ask if the person is choking and if they need help. Get the person to stand for better leverage, and stand behind him or her. Make a fist with your dominant hand, and place the thumb side on the person's mid-abdomen, just next to the chest. Put your other hand over that hand, and push your hands in sharply. Repeat until the object comes out.

THE FIRST AID KIT EVERY HOME NEEDS

At home, first aid kits come in handy to treat everything from minor injuries to more serious ones. Your home kit must be able to help you take care of cuts, abrasions, burns, stings, splinters, sprains, fever, nasal congestion, cough, sore throat, and gastrointestinal problems. What should you have? Sterile gloves, sanitizer, gauze, adhesive tape, adhesive bandages, an antiseptic salve, antibiotic ointment, scissors and tweezers, elastic wraps, pain relievers, a thermometer, cough medicine, skin rash cream, cream/spray for sprains/stings, eye drops, etc. Don't forget to check expiration dates and replace any items that are outdated. Maintaining a list of contents in the kit can help keep track of missing or expired items.

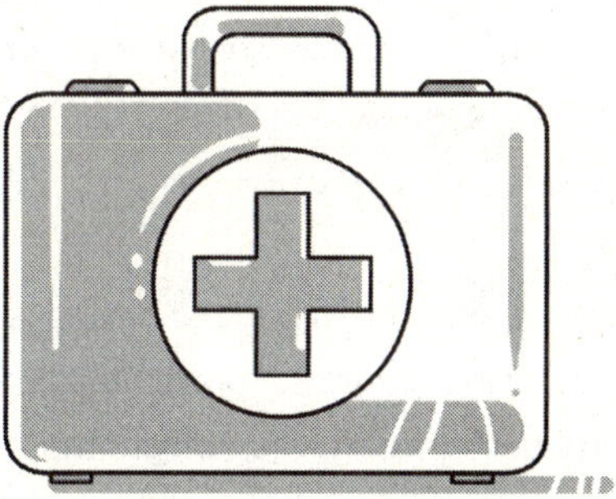

63.

RECOGNIZE MEDICAL EMERGENCIES

It's important to be able to recognize medical emergencies to help provide adequate and essential care immediately. This could be the difference between life and death.

How

- **Heart attack:** A person might be having a heart attack if they're experiencing tightness, pressure, pain, or a squeezing sensation in their chest/arms, which then spreads to the neck, back, or jaw; shortness of breath or cold sweat, nausea, indigestion, heartburn, or abdominal pain are other symptoms.
- **Low blood sugar:** Signs of low blood sugar (hypoglycaemia) include sweating, chills, and clamminess, shakiness and nervousness, confusion, light-headedness, dizziness, and a rapid heartbeat. Raise your blood sugar by eating a small snack – a banana, apple, orange, a glass of juice, or two tablespoons of raisins.

- **Stroke:** Recognize a stroke by the **FAST** warning signs – **F**ace drooping, **A**rm weakness, **S**lurred speech, **T**ime to call (an expert). Other indications include a severe headache without any known cause and difficulty seeing in one or both eyes.

- **Blood pressure changes:** Dizziness, nervousness, sweating, facial flushing, trouble sleeping, and blood spots in eyes may indicate a hypertensive (high BP) episode. Recognize low BP (hypotension) by these symptoms – dizziness, nausea, blurred vision, dehydration, and cold/clammy skin.
- See a medical expert in case you experience any of these symptoms.

64.

BECOME A PRO AT CPR

Cardiopulmonary resuscitation (CPR) may be needed unexpectedly in cases of cardiac arrests or drowning. Even knowing the basics of hands-only CPR can help save a life.

How

- After calling for an ambulance, place one of your hands on top of the other and clasp them together.
- With the heel of the hands and straight elbows, push hard and fast in the centre of the chest to a tune that is at least 100 beats per minute. Think *Staying Alive* by the Bee Gees.

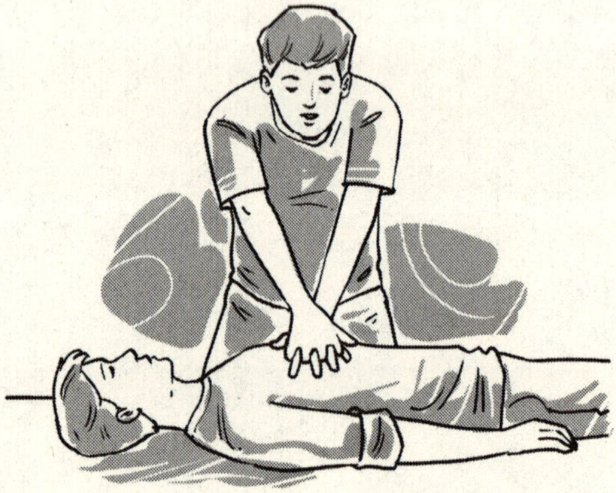

- Follow 30 chest compressions up with 2 rescue breaths.

- Make sure the mouth is clear, tilt the head back slightly, and lift the chin. Pinch the nose shut, place your mouth fully over the person's, and blow in air to make the chest rise. If the chest does not rise with the first breath, tilt the head again. Continue till help is at hand.

65.

HOME REMEDIES FOR HEADACHES

So little time, so much to do. Is it a wonder that headaches have become part and parcel of our existence? But stay away from pill-popping to ease the niggling ache and try these time-tested home remedies instead.

How

- **Massage the ache away:** Working on a few specific pressure points can help address the pain. Begin by stimulating the third eye – the pressure point between the eyebrows – and either apply constant pressure or gently massage in a circular motion. Move to the pair of pressure points on the inside of each eyebrow. Use both your index fingers to apply equal pressure to the points where the nose bridge meets the brow bone.
- **Use the hot-cold technique:** Muscle tension headaches can be treated with hot and/or cold compresses. Put ice in a plastic bag and slip into a folded handkerchief for a quick cold pack;

place on your forehead and/or cheeks. After five minutes, use a hot pack for on the back of your neck or forehead for relief.

- **Drink a cup of herbal tea:** Apart from warmth and comfort, a steaming cup of herbal tea can also offer pain-relieving effects. Sip on a tea that enhances relaxation, such as chamomile, ginger, and dandelion.
- **Use scented oils:** Certain smells can trigger positive responses in the brain and are known to soothe headaches. Dab a couple of drops of peppermint, eucalyptus, or lavender essential oil on the inside of your wrist to ease the pain.
- **Try breathing exercises:** Deep breathing can often help ease tense muscles and relieve headache pain. Sit comfortably and take slow, rhythmic breaths, breathing in for five seconds and then out for five seconds. As you relax, your muscle tightness reduces.
- **Get some magnesium:** Magnesium relaxes blood vessels and can reduce headaches. Apart from an oral magnesium citrate supplement (only on prescription), you can try consuming magnesium-rich foods, such as bananas, nuts, seeds, dark chocolate, and cocoa.

66.

DIY MENTHOL CHEST RUB

Tired of the stuffy nose and congestion in chest? Try this homemade chest rub to clear out your airways.

What you need

- ✓ 250 ml carrier oil
- ✓ 1 tsp menthol crystals
- ✓ 30 gms beeswax
- ✓ 20 drops eucalyptus essential oil
- ✓ 10 drops peppermint essential oil
- ✓ 10 drops cinnamon essential oil

Time > 30 minutes

How

- Put the carrier oil and beeswax in a double boiler until the beeswax melts. Remove from heat immediately.
- Add the menthol crystals and essential oils, stir till dissolved, and quickly pour into small glass jars. Cover the jars loosely so the oils don't waft away.
- Seal the caps after the rub cools down. Play with the amount of beeswax – using less will create a runny rub; using it all will create a proper balm.

67.

MAKE A HEAT PACK

You need a hot compression treatment and don't have one of those fancy gel packs at home. What do you do? Make your own reusable heat pack in a few minutes.

What you need **Time** < 10 minutes

✓ An old sock
✓ 1 cup rice
✓ Needle and thread

How

- Loosely fill the old sock with rice and stitch up the end. Add a ribbon to gussy it up if you must, but it works well without.
- Pop the heat pack into the microwave and heat for 2 minutes before applying on the affected area.

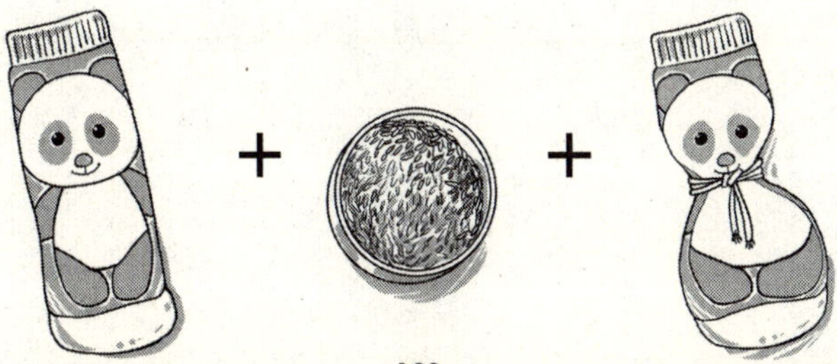

68.

DEAL WITH BLEMISHES, BURNS, CUTS AND RASHES

Bring out the masala dabba if you swipe at a finger while cutting veggies or spot a tiny blemish.

Try: Turmeric

How

- Apply directly to the skin in case of a cut; mix with water, milk or aloe vera to make a thin paste and spread on blemishes, burns, and acne.
- The antibacterial and anti-fungal nature of this spice makes it ideal to use in case of cuts, scrapes, sunburns, acne, and more.

69.

TACKLE SKIN INFECTION, ECZEMA AND DRYNESS

The sun, wind, and rain can play havoc with your skin. Rifle through the kitchen cabinets for easy remedies.

Try: Oats

How

- Add powdered oatmeal to your bath water or use in a homemade scrub with milk, honey, and turmeric.
- The presence of linoleic oil, oleic acid, and avenanthramides reduces the level of cytokines, which can cause inflammation.

Try: Honey, aloe vera, and coconut oil

How

- Extract aloe-vera gel from a leaf, mix with honey and coconut oil to create a homemade skin balm.
- Apply before bath, leave on for 10 minutes, and wash off.

70.

EASE A SORE THROAT

A change in season and you're bound to feel *gale me khich khich*. Keep a sore throat at bay, the easy way.

Try: Honey, lemon, and pepper

How

- Mix a tablespoon of honey with the juice of half a lemon, add quarter teaspoon of pepper powder, and suck on it slowly. Do it thrice a day at least.
- The honey soothes and disinfects, the lemon calms inflamed tissues, while the black pepper stimulates circulation and encourages healing.

Try: Baking soda/turmeric and warm water gargles

How

- Mix a glass warm water with a teaspoon of baking soda or turmeric and gargle to rid yourself of a sore throat.

71.

EASY HACKS FOR COUGH AND COLD

The cure for the common cough and cold continues to elude doctors, so start natural treatments as soon as they make an appearance.

Try: Ginger, garlic, honey, and turmeric

How

- Mix a tablespoon of crushed ginger and garlic with a pinch of turmeric, and a tablespoon of honey to make a cough syrup.
- The golden spice treats inflammation and related pain, while the ginger blocks the formation of certain inflammatory compounds and breaks down existing inflammation.
- The garlic decreases the frequency of colds, while the natural antibacterial and anti-inflammatory properties of honey soothe the throat.

Try: Ginger, cayenne pepper, apple cider vinegar, and honey

How

- Mix two tablespoons each of cider vinegar, honey and water, and add a quarter teaspoon of grated ginger and cayenne pepper, in a small glass jar.
- Shake the watery syrup each time before consuming – 4 to 5 times a day.

Try: Mustard

How

- Mustard plasters have been used for centuries to sweat out the flu, cough, cold, and pneumonia. Mix 2 tablespoons of ground mustard with 4 tablespoons flour, and add warm water to make a thick paste.
- Spread over an old piece of cloth to create a pack, and place on your chest pack-side down.
- Top with a hot water bottle and relax for about 20 minutes.

BONUS HACK

RELIEVE CONGESTION

When you put a 'D' at the end of 'Fine' you're not fine, as Ross told Monica on *Friends*. So, deal with that congestion STAT.

Try: A warm compress and eucalyptus oil

How

- Apply a warm compress, with a few drops of eucalyptus oil, to open up nasal passages, and ease a clogged nose and congestion.

Try: Onion juice with lemon and honey

How

- Mix freshly extracted onion juice with lemon juice, honey, and warm water.
- Onions contain quercetin, which is said to help flush out mucus and prevent further build up. Its antimicrobial properties also prevent infections – so drink up!

72.

BREAK A FEVER

Over-the-counter medications can lower fevers, but try these home remedies before popping a pill.

Try: Ghee

How

- This isn't just an old wives' tale. A ghee massage can be therapeutic and can even help break a fever.
- Rub warm ghee on the soles of your feet to bring down your body temperature.

Try: Apple cider vinegar

How

- Apple cider vinegar has numerous health benefits, including antimicrobial and antioxidant effects. Add 2-5 tablespoons to a large bowl of tepid water, and bathe your arms and legs.
- The acidic solution speeds up heat loss as it evaporates off the skin, and slowly brings down the body temperature. However, visit a doctor immediately if the fever persists.

73.

RELIEVE AN EARACHE

An earache can make you fussy and irritable, but it's possible to dim the niggling pain.

Try: Garlic oil

How

- Warm a couple of tablespoons of coconut oil with three cloves of crushed garlic in a pan over low heat.
- Swirl till just fragrant – not smoking or bubbling.
- Pour a few drops in each ear thrice a day. Garlic, which has antiviral, antibacterial, and anti-fungal properties, has for long been used as a natural remedy for ear issues.

Try: Hot/cold pack

How

- Holding a heating pad or a hot cloth against your ear for 15 minutes can relax the muscles, improve blood flow, and ease pain.
- Using an ice pack may reduce any inflammation and numb the pain, providing relief for a while. Visit a doctor if the pain persists.

74.

TACKLE A TOOTHACHE

Agatha Christie's Hercule Poirot wasn't immune to toothache, then how can we lesser mortals not be affected by it? These remedies can help tackle tooth twinges.

Try: Salt water and cold compress

How

- Mix half a teaspoon of salt in a glass of warm water and use as a mouthwash. Salt water works as a natural disinfectant, and can help reduce inflammation and heal oral wounds.
- Follow this up with a cold compress application, which constricts the blood vessels, and reduces swelling and inflammation.

Try: Clove oil

How

- Cloves, which contain eugenol, a natural antiseptic, have been used to relieve tooth pain for centuries. Dab a small amount of clove oil onto a cotton ball and apply to the affected area several times a day.

- You can also crush a few cloves, mix with a bit of water, and apply the paste on the sore tooth/gum. Visit your dentist if there's no relief.

SMART TIPS

- Get acute tooth pain under control by massaging an ice pack over the affected region till it feels numb.
- Massage ice over the flesh between the thumb and index finger of the hand on the same side as the painful tooth for relief.

75.

Reduce Nausea

Nausea can be kept under control with some kitchen remedies. Say yes to that road trip or plane journey!

Try: Ginger

How

- Slice a piece into thin strips, sprinkle with ample salt and sugar, and add a tablespoon of lemon juice.
- Place in a glass jar and refrigerate for up to 3 months.
- Consume whenever nausea strikes.

Try: Peppermint oil

How

- Rub a few drops on the inside of your wrist and inhale.

Try: Spices

How

- A spice tea made from a mix of fennel and cumin seeds, cinnamon, and cardamom can reduce the feeling of queasiness and leave you feeling refreshed.

76.

TACKLE GASTROINTESTINAL PROBLEMS

Peace in the stomach translates to peace in the head. So tummy trouble – no matter what kind – must be dealt with pronto.

Indigestion

Try: Ginger and salt

How

- In Ayurveda, indigestion is caused by weak "digestive fire'. Consuming a ginger-salt mix (a small piece of fresh grated ginger with a pinch of salt) can help fuel this fire.

Try: Spice tea

How

- Follow up your meal with a tea brewed with fennel, caraway, carom, and dill seeds for immediate relief. Many of these spices have carminative properties, helping relieve gas, bloating, and other dyspepsia-related symptoms.

Diarrhoea

Try: Fenugreek seeds

How

- Mix a tablespoon of fenugreek seeds (powder also works) with a tablespoon of curd, which contains probiotics, and consume. The high mucilage content of these seeds helps cure diarrhoea.

Constipation

Try: Milk and ghee

How

- Add a teaspoon of ghee to a glass of hot milk and consume at bedtime to make going in the morning easy as pie. This traditional Indian home remedy has been used for aeons.

Try: Sesame seeds

How

- Chomp down on a tablespoon of sesame seeds and follow up with a glass of warm water at bedtime. The high fibre content in the seeds facilitates bowel movements.

Try: Castor oil

How

- Take a tablespoon of the oil – used as a laxative for thousands of years – and wait for nature's call! The main fatty acid in castor oil, ricinoleic acid, binds with the receptors on the smooth muscle cells of the intestinal walls, causing the muscles to contract and push out stool.

SMART TIPS

- Chew on a teaspoonful (mix some salt in, if you need) of carom seeds and wash down with water, or mix with a pinch of salt and warm water to tackle indigestion and stomach pain.
- Suck on a peppermint candy or chew on flavoured gum to enhance digestion and soothe an upset stomach. The presence of menthol and methyl salicylate have a calming and numbing effects on the gastrointestinal tract.
- Our grandparents knew the best and easiest way to ease constipation: squatting. Even if most homes no longer have Indian-style toilets, placing a small stool under the legs can help raise your knees your above hips when in the loo.

77.

TACKLE BUG BITES

Stepping out in the summer is often akin to sending bugs an invite to bite. What can you do after your skin has been punctured by these pesky critters?

Try: Honey

How

- A coat of honey, renowned for its anti-inflammatory properties, can soothe the affected area and reduce itching.

Try: Milk and water

How

- This age-old solution involves mixing equal parts milk and water, and dabbing it on the bite. The protein in the milk soothes the itch.

Try: Coconut oil

How

- A layer of coconut oil soothes itchy skin, and protects the affected area from dust and dirt. Its antibacterial properties can hasten healing.

Try: Toothpaste

How

- The menthol in most toothpastes creates a cooling sensation and numbs the affected area, providing instant relief. The astringent properties reduce swelling.

Try: Banana peel

How

- The peel that you bin has a high antioxidant content and can soothe inflamed bug bites, especially mosquito bites.
- Place the peel, fruit-side down, on the bite and rub gently until the itching/burning calms down.

78.

DEAL WITH INSOMNIA

Staying up when everyone else has entered the Land of Nod feels like the worst punishment. Fortunately, you don't have to.

Try: Sole massage and nutmeg milk

How

- According to Ayurveda, all 'nadis' begin in the scalp and end in the soles of the feet. Giving your soles an extended foot rub with warm oil can soothe feelings of anxiety and help you sleep better. Drink a cup of warm milk infused with nutmeg, which releases serotonin and calms nerves, to induce sleep faster.

Try: Lavender

How

- This essential oil delivers a sense of calm, improves mood, reduces pain, and promotes sleep. Splash a couple of drops on your pillow or use via an aromatherapy diffuser in the room for improved sleep.

Try: Chamomile tea

How

- The calming effects of chamomile tea are attributed to apigenin, an antioxidant that binds with the receptors in the brain that may decrease anxiety and initiate sleep.

Try: Magnesium

How

- The presence of this mineral helps relax muscles, reduce stress, and encourage a healthy sleep-wake cycle. Opt for magnesium-rich foods an hour before bedtime: a mug of warm milk, a banana, dark chocolate, nuts, seeds, or whole grains.

79.

HERBAL INFUSIONS AND DECOCTIONS

Water is the commonly used medium to extract the goodness from herbs in the form of teas, infusions, and decoctions. Herbal teas, are technically tisanes: infusions are usually made with flowers or leaves and can be had hot or cold; decoctions, on the other hand, are made by simmering roots, barks, seeds, and more in water. Each of these methods has benefits and breaks down the plant constituents in a different manner. Hot infusions 'burst' open the cell walls, while cold ones coax them open gently to draw out vitamins, enzymes, and more. Use glass or ceramic containers when making these concoctions.

Make a hot infusion

Try: Chamomile, rose petals, mint, tulsi, lemongrass, ginger, nettle, rosemary, thyme, hibiscus

How

- Place a teaspoon of the herbs of your choice in a teapot or mug.
- Pour water that's been heated to a boil and submerge the herbs.
- Cover to contain volatile oils, if any, and let steep for 5 minutes.

Chamomile calms nerves and regulates diabetes; rose improves sleep and betters mood swings; tulsi prevents respiratory disorders and reduces stress; ginger tackles digestive issues, eases headaches and is anti-inflammatory.

Make a cold infusion

Try: Liquorice root, peppermint, chamomile, rose buds, lavender

How

- Place the loose herbs – fresh or dry – in a clean glass jar, top off with cold water, and allow to infuse overnight.

Liquorice root soothes sore throat, betters digestion and protects against infection; peppermint eases digestion, enhances energy and helps with headaches; lavender soothes anxiety, promotes sleep and skin health.

Make a decoction

Try: Ginger, liquorice root, ashwagandha, fennel, cumin, cinnamon

How

- Place the herbs and seeds in a small saucepan, add water, and slowly heat. Let it simmer for 15 minutes and strain.

Fennel helps fight infections, promotes sleep and is packed with antioxidants; Cinnamon reduces inflammation, improves brain function and boosts metabolism.

80.

IMMUNITEA TO BOOST THE IMMUNE SYSTEM

Keep your immune system – the moat that keeps your body safe – in top condition by mixing together a blend of immunity-enhancing ingredients.

What you need **Time** > 10 minutes

✓ ½ tsp ground turmeric
✓ ¼ tsp ground cinnamon
✓ ½ tsp ground ashwagandha
✓ ½ tsp grated ginger
✓ 2-3 strips lemongrass
✓ 7-8 tulsi leaves

How

- Add water to a saucepan and mix in the ingredients.
- Bring to a boil and let simmer for 7-10 minutes.
- Strain and serve.

81.

GOODNIGHT BREW

Forget the nightcaps that are now in the market, and make a homemade one instead. It is easy to put together, and has no chemicals and preservatives. Sip slowly on a warm mug of this tea and enjoy your zzzs.

What you need

Time > 10 minutes

- ✓ ½ tsp ground cinnamon
- ✓ ½ tsp ground nutmeg
- ✓ ¼ tsp allspice
- ✓ 3-4 cloves
- ✓ 1 orange peel
- ✓ 1 tsp honey

How

- Put all the ingredients in a saucepan, cover with water, and bring to a boil.
- Let it simmer for 10 minutes.
- Strain and serve.

82.

SIMPLE DESK EXERCISES

A sedentary lifestyle does more harm to our bodies than we realize. Prolonged sitting is one of the root causes of numerous serious health concerns, including obesity, diabetes, arthritis, cardiovascular disease, brittle bones, colon cancer, back pain, deep vein-thrombosis, depression and dementia. It's easy to undo the damage desk jobs do by building in small exercises into your routine.

How

- **March in place:** Stand comfortably and march in place, trying to push towards the ceiling with your palms up. Hold one-litre water bottles in both hands to increase intensity.
- **Flap those arms:** Stand with your arms by your sides, palms facing behind you. Keep your arms straight and flap them backwards for 5-10 seconds. Release and repeat.
- **Lunge sideways:** Place both hands on the edge of your desk, shoulder-width apart. Ensure your feet and knees are together; take a large step with your right foot to the right side and lunge toward the floor. Repeat on the other side.

- **Lift your heels:** This easy exercise gets the blood moving to the soles of your feet. Sit tall and lift your heels off the floor; alternate with a standing version.

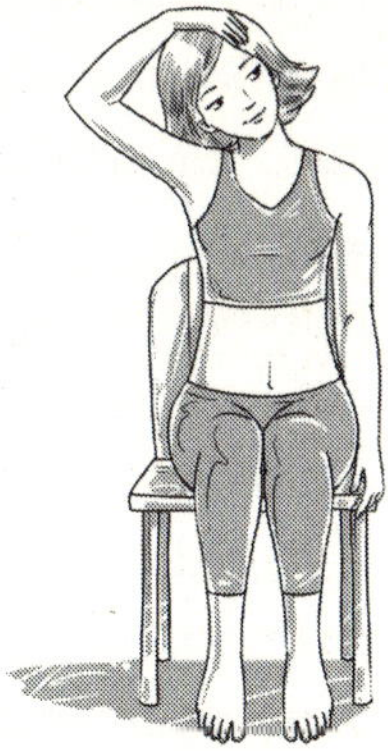

- **Stretch your neck:** Sit straight and, with one hand, grip the seat of your chair. Reach over your head with the other hand. Your aim is to try and grab the opposite ear as you stretch your neck by leaning towards the arm over your head.
- **Relax your wrists:** Extend one arm in front of you, palms facing upwards. Use the other hand to pull the hand straight down at the wrist and hold. Repeat with the other hand.

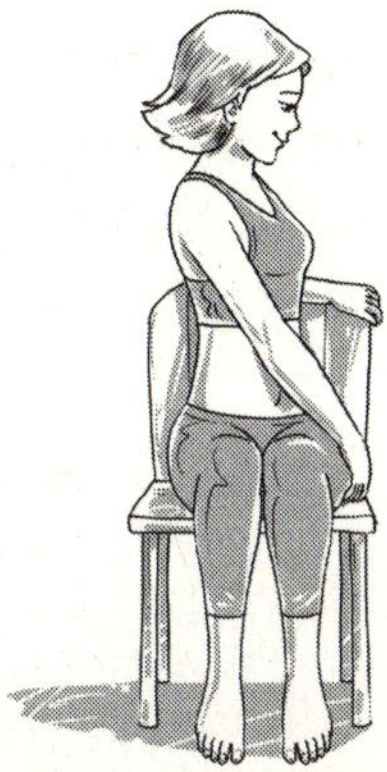

- **Twist in the chair:** Sit on the chair with your back straight and tall, and the soles of your feet placed flat on the floor. Take a deep breath and exhale while twisting your body left from the abs. Stay in position for a few seconds. Repeat on the other side.
- **Try a desk squat:** Place feet together and bend your knees slightly till your thighs are almost parallel to the ground. Raise your arms towards the desk as you bend.
- **Work the abs:** Take a deep breath and tighten the abdominal muscles, imagining that you want your navel to touch the back. Hold for 10-15 seconds and release.

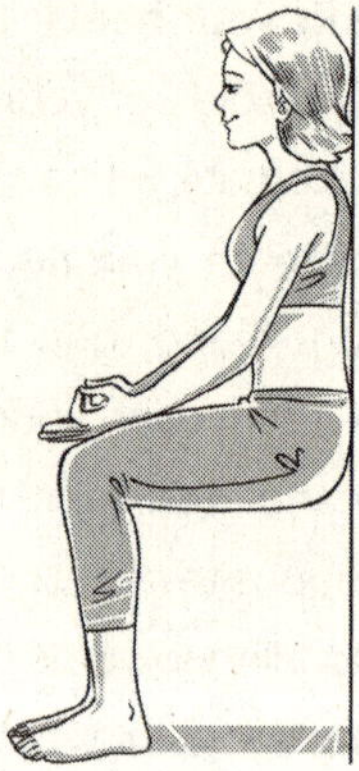

- **Use the wall:** Stand straight with your back against the wall. Bend your knees and slide down the wall until your thighs are parallel to the floor. Hold for 30-60 seconds.
- **Tone the triceps:** Sit at the edge of a sturdy chair and grip the sides with both hands. Keeping your feet a step or two away, straighten your arms and lift the body. Bend your arms to reach a 90-degree angle; your body must dip down now. Repeat 5-6 times.
- **Shrug your shoulders:** Roll your shoulders back till you feel your shoulder blades squeezed together. Hold for 10-15 seconds and release.
- **Try leg raises:** Straighten one leg ahead of you while seated and hold for five seconds. Lower to the ground without touching the floor. Repeat with the other leg/try both together.

SMART TIPS

- For every hour you sit at your desk, which puts recurring pressure on the base of your spine, work standing for at least 10 minutes. Over time and with practice, you can increase this to up to half an hour.
- Taking the stairs gives you the same short-term energy boost as half a cup of coffee – so make sure you incorporate it into each day.

83.

EXERCISES TO MAINTAIN EYE HEALTH

There is no getting away from screen time. Phones, telly, laptops, tablets – screens are everywhere and your eyes are under duress to keep working hard through the day. Take these easy steps to keep an eye on your ocular health and ensure good vision.

How

- **Change focus:** Switching focus between objects that are near and far exercises your eye muscles and should be done seated. Hold your pointer finger a few inches away from your eye and focus on it. Slowly move your finger away, holding focus. Look away for a moment and return focus on the finger, slowly bringing it back toward your eye. Repeat 3-5 times.
- **Quick focus change:** Hold your thumb about 10 inches away from your face and focus on it for 15-18 seconds. Then look at an object about 20 feet away and focus on it for 15-18 seconds. Return focus to your thumb. Repeat 3-5 times.
- **Flex your eye muscles:** To strengthen your ocular muscles, sit down, face forward, and look straight ahead. Look up without

moving your head and then look down. Do this 10 times. Next, look as far right as you can without moving your head and then to the left again without moving your head. Do 10 repetitions.

- **Draw the figure eight:** Stare at a blank wall and imagine a large figure 8, tilted on its side on the surface. Trace the path of this number with your eyes, without moving your head. Do one way for 1 minute and then the other for 1 minute.
- **20-20-20 rule:** Look away from your screen every 20 minutes and focus on something that is 20 feet away for 20 seconds.
- **Blink regularly:** Blinking often helps lubricate your eyes naturally, which prevents dry eye. If they feel too dry, try using over-the-counter lubricating eye drops.

SMART TIPS

- Use palming to soothe tired eyes at the end of a long working day. Close your eyes and place both palms so they cover your eyes. The fingers should be on your forehead and the base of the palm on your cheekbone. *Do not put pressure.* Palm for two minutes.
- Hot and cold compresses can help soothe your eyes. Dip one end of a hand towel in hot water and place on your eyes. After 10 seconds, place a cold compress. Do this routine 3-5 times.
- Triphala can also help relieve tired, screen-weary eyes. Soak a small spoonful in water in a clay vessel/matka for 8-10 hours, and wash eyes with this twice a day.

84.

PRIORITIZE YOUR MENTAL HEALTH

The World Health Organization defines mental health as 'a state of well-being in which the individual realizes his or her own abilities, can cope with the normal stresses of life, can work productively and fruitfully, and is able to make a contribution to his or her community'. Mental health influences how we think, feel, behave, and rally in daily life, which makes it important for us to prioritize it – especially in today's extra-busy and turbulent times.

How

- **Love yourself best:** Like Geet said in *Jab We Met*, 'Mai apni favourite hoon'. But words aren't enough, so focus on every aspect of you. Eat a healthy diet, get enough sleep, and make time for exercise. A morning routine that ranks exercise among your early to-dos ensures that you don't skip this important step. Run, walk, jog ... Whatever you do best, to get a morning high.

- **Get a mental workout:** The brain is the control centre of the body, which means it should be kept in tip-top shape. Keep your mental faculties sharp by doing things that force your brain to change perspective and think differently – use your non-dominant hand more frequently, learn a new language, try a new kind of exercise, play games, learn a new word every day, do puzzles, and do routine things (brush your teeth, take a shower, button your shirt) with your eyes closed.
- **Cut out alcohol and cigarettes:** It may seem tough, but take small steps in this direction. Boozing and smoking never did anyone any good, and only offer temporary relief from stress and unhappiness. Divert your energies elsewhere, and seek support – from family and friends or professionals – when you need it.
- **Laugh till you drop:** Those uncles and aunties who laugh themselves silly after yoga knew a secret: laughing is no joke! Humour and laughter activate the brain's reward and pleasure centres, generating happy emotions and relaxing the mind. If you can't laugh at will, watch a funny show or read a comic strip.
- **Connect with friends:** Friends are the family we choose and can keep us grounded, give us perspective when we need it, and help us manage the problems that life throws at us. Instead of blocking them out, reach out to close friends for emotional support that can help you feel supported, valued, and loved.
- **Take a deep breath:** When it all seems a bit too much and you don't know what to do, step away and do a simple breathing exercise. Close your eyes and take ten deep breaths. For each one, count to five as you inhale, hold it for a count of five, and then exhale for another five. Breathing deeply sends a message to your brain to calm down and relax.

SMART TIPS

- Planning a getaway, even if you are not going on one, helps improve your mood. Drawing up plans for a vacation gives you something to look forward to (even if it's not actually happening) and can boost your overall happiness for more than a week.
- Stepping into the outdoors in the early morning to enjoy 15 minutes of sunshine (after applying sunscreen) can help as sunlight synthesizes Vitamin D, which experts believe is a mood elevator.
- A digital detox – a full 24 hours with no computer, phone, internet, or telly – can work wonders. It can reduce stress, boost your self-esteem, make you more empathetic and creative, help you think more clearly, and improve sleep.
- Make it a habit to track gratitude and achievement. Journaling seems like a big task, but all you need to do is write down three things you were grateful for and three things you were able to accomplish each day.
- Meredith Grey sure knew what she was doing when she and her pals lay on the grass in the sun. Now recognized as 'grounding', this simple act can reduce stress and anxiety, and enhance sleep. If you don't have access to a lawn, consider walking barefoot in a public garden!

85.

LEARN TO MEDITATE

The hullaballoo around meditation may have started in the West somewhat recently, but our rishis have lived by the mindfulness meditation mantra for centuries. The practice is all about focusing your attention inwards, to induce a state of deep relaxation, and become more aware of thoughts and feelings. Taking a few minutes to focus the mind each day can reduce stress and pain, increase calmness and clarity, and promote happiness.

The very thought of sitting calmly and being one with our thoughts – that huge, bottomless pit – appears formidable, but it's possible to train ourselves to do it.

How

- Find a quiet place to meditate and ensure that there's nothing to disturb you. Leave your phone in another room, if you must, and sit in a comfortable position on the floor. Sit upright, but relaxed.

- Close your eyes and try to focus only on one thing: your breathing. Breathe gently, and pay attention to each inhale and exhale. Another way to go is a 'body scan' – begin with your toes and go all the way up to your hair, focusing on the sensations in each part of your body.
- Experts say there is no such thing as a good or bad meditation; there's only awareness and non-awareness. Distractions are a given because the mind is a hotbed of thoughts. Try and bring your attention back to your breath when your mind wanders. This is one of the best ways to learn to quell your mind and focus on the moment.

- Begin by doing 2-minute span of meditation and work your way up to 5 to 10 minutes each day. Some people go up to 30-45 minutes once they learn the technique, but figure out what works best for you. Meditating at the same time every day helps make it a habit.

BONUS HACK

UPLIFT YOUR MOOD

Voltaire famously said that the most important decision you make is to be in a good mood. Banish the blues!

Try: Cinnamon

How

- Egyptians used cinnamon as early as 2000 BC to treat different health conditions. But research shows that even smelling cinnamon enhances cognitive performance and uplifts the mood. Just pop a few cinnamon sticks into boiling water and steep on the stovetop. The fragrance is sure to quell the blues.

Try: Dark chocolate

How

- A couple of squares of dark chocolate – 75 per cent or more – ups the serotonin levels in the brain.
- The presence of flavonols increases blood flow to the brain, while the amino acid tryptophan induces a feeling of calm. But all said and done, it's the feeling of having had dessert that gives an instant shot of happiness.

SECTION 5

REUSE AND RECYCLE

'There is no such thing as away. When we throw anything away it must go somewhere.'

— Annie Leonard

Multiple cardboard boxes that Amazon delivered your order in, a plastic water bottle, a squeezed-out tube of toothpaste, old knick-knacks that no longer look cute, vegetable scraps, leftovers ... Have you ever taken a closer look at the trash that goes out of your home each day?

Everything we use in our daily life – from the toothbrush in the morning to the chamomile tea sachet in the night – must go somewhere once we're done with it. These things don't just disappear simply because they are 'out of sight, out of mind' – even though you and I would really like them to. No fairy godmother can magically make all the waste disappear and leave us with a clean slate!

That waste ends up in landfills, breaking down at snail's pace and releasing gases that play a huge role in climate change. Many things, including certain kinds of plastics, survive for aeons without disintegrating and add to the waste acreage. Every item of daily use has an associated environmental cost, which includes the energy used to produce it and the impact it leaves when dumped.

It's startling to see the amount of trash that every household manages to churn out each day. India, which accounts for about 18 per cent of the world's population, is responsible for 12 per cent of global municipal solid waste generation.[1] According to a

2018 World Bank report, the country is the world's highest waste-generating nation, with Delhi topping the list.[2] A report published in *The Print* cited a World Bank study revealing that according to a 2016 estimate, India's annual waste generated is likely to touch 543.3 million tonnes by 2050.[3]

Let's break it down further.

An average Indian generates about 600 gms of waste per day as of now; this is slated to hit 900 gms each day by 2050. Much of this waste, which includes food discards, could be reduced, reused, or recycled to help create a cleaner and greener world. The stats are so staggering that it's easy to get overwhelmed.

How can I help? How much can my solitary efforts contribute? IMMENSELY.

If every person decides to do their bit to give back to the environment, by adopting the 'reduce, reuse, and recycle' mantra, we would leave the world a much better place.

Life, as it tends to, has come a full circle, and the answer to this particular what-to-do can be found in our past. It's a fact that long before the three Rs became fashionable, our forebears – those who ran those homesteads – were living a green life by adopting a 'waste not, want not' mantra. They reused and repurposed clothes, food, kitchen items, fabrics, and more, were thrifty with almost everything, and made recycling a part of every single thing they did. Clothes were handed down amongst cousins, leftovers were recrafted into new meals, school snacks were packed in steel tiffins, old towels and sheets were transformed into foot mats and dusters, and cracked cups and jars got a new life as planters.

Unlike today's recycling crafters, many of who go out and buy things to use and upcycle, our great-grandmas were hardwired to reuse and recycle. Their thrifty habits – often scoffed at – are now life goals!

Change is around us. According to a Nielson report, 73 per cent of global consumers say they would definitely or probably change their consumption habits to reduce their impact on the environment.[4]

But that's not enough. No, sirree!

Smart decisions on what we buy will be the beginning, but these need to be followed up with ways to extend the life cycle of every single item. Reuse things, repurpose them, give them away, and make sure they are recycled. Living a green lifestyle may sound tough, but these simple hacks can help you get started. Stick with it and the environment will thank you. And so will your wallet!

The 7 Rs

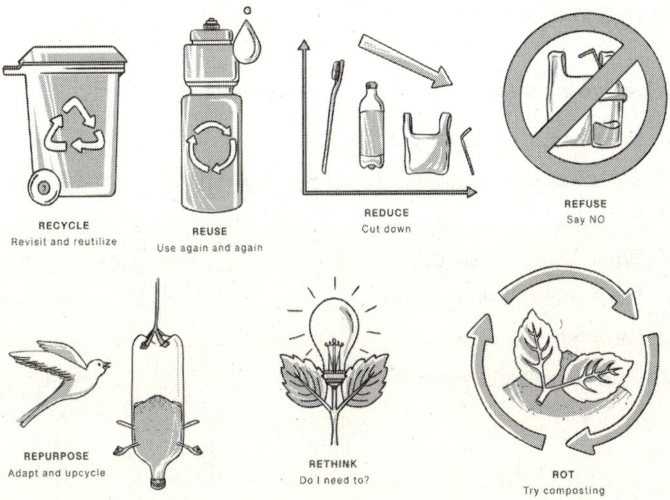

86.

REUSABLE BEESWAX WRAPS

Environment-friendly kitchen swaps are all the rage these days. Join the movement by DIYing these pliable beeswax wraps to cover up foods, snacks, and bowls of leftovers in the fridge. Bye-bye plastic lids, cling film, and foil! Rinse clean with cold water and a dab of mild soap, and reuse.

What you need **Time** < 1 hour

- ✓ Cosmetic-grade beeswax pellets
- ✓ Scraps of cotton fabric
- ✓ Scissors
- ✓ Brush (that can be discarded)
- ✓ Parchment/baking paper
- ✓ Baking tray
- ✓ Velcro/buttons/elastic

How

- Preheat the oven to 200°F (95°C). Cut the fabric into sizes that will fit your baking tray and will cover majority of bowls – 7x14 inches for a snack pouch, 12x12 inches for bowl covers, and 14x14 inches to fit in sandwiches.
- Line a baking tray with parchment paper and place the fabric on it. Evenly distribute a liberal amount of beeswax pellets over the fabric, including the edges. Use a fresh piece of parchment each time you make a new wrap.
- Put in the oven for 5-8 minutes. Bring out the tray after the pellets melt and use the brush to spread the wax over the fabric evenly. Let dry. Remove and hang to dry some more.
- Once the beeswax has set, you can add buttons, Velcro, or a band of elastic to create sandwich wraps, snack bags and bowl covers, respectively.

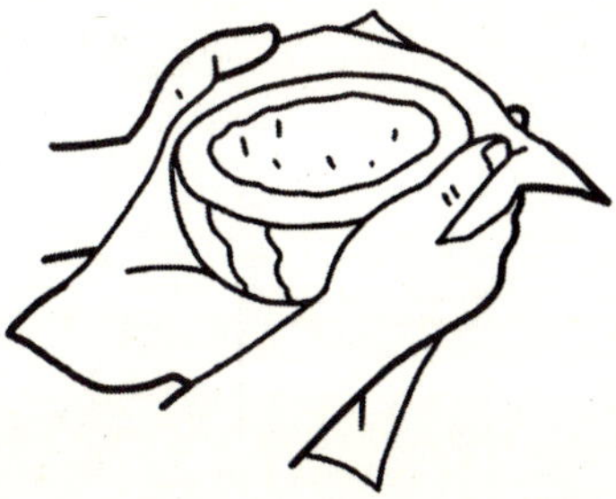

87.

TAWASHI DISH SCRUBBER

The history of the Tawashi goes back hundreds of years. Traditionally, rice straw was used to make early versions of this cleaning brush; it was was replaced by palm fibres in the 20th century. In today's times, why not use orphaned socks to make dish scrubbers that are zero waste, washable, and long-lasting?

What you need

✓ Wooden board and hammer

✓ 20 nails

✓ 2 old socks

Time < 30 minutes

Makes 1

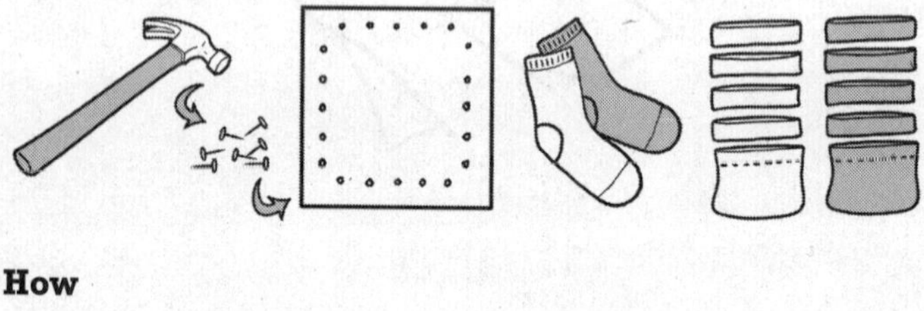

How

- Draw a square about 18x18 cm on one side of the board and make a 2.5x2.5 inches grid. Hammer in nails along the grid.

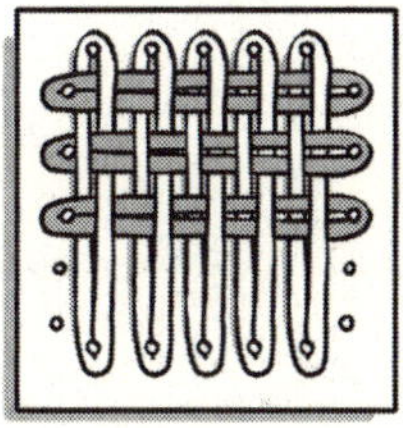

- Cut the socks (not woollen) into 12 strips of the same size. Pull on them to distend and then place them on six nails in one direction. Place the remaining 6 strips in the other direction, so as to make a checkerboard pattern by passing over the strips already in place.
- Unhook the first strip on the left from its nail and then the next one. Insert it into the first. Let go of the first, keeping only the second in hand and repeat. Continue with all the loops. Pull hard on the last link or make a knot to secure. The open loop can be used as a hook.

- Use to scrub dishes that need light scouring. Toss into the wash after a day's work.

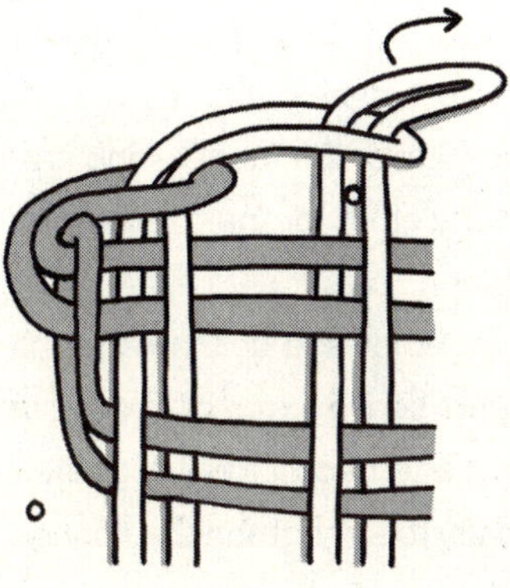

88.

UNSPONGE

No kitchen can do without sponges to wipe spills and clean up. But those plastic polyfoam sponges we use to mop up can be very hard on the environment. Why not make your own reusable sponges from remnants of terry cloth and cotton fabric?

What you need

✓ Thick cotton fabric, for the top

✓ An old towel/napkin, for the middle

✓ Muslin or thin cotton fabric, for the bottom

Time < 1 hour

Makes 2-3

How

- Cut the fabric into squares, about 7x7 inches, or rectangles, about 6x8 inches. Layer the fabric – one layer of cotton for the top, a layer of terry cloth for the middle, and a layer of muslin for the lower layer.
- Pin the layers together and sew a half-inch seam allowance all the way around. Leave a gap of about 2 inches on one side. Turn it inside out and backstitch it together. You can also run stitches diagonally to strengthen the sponge.
- These can be thrown into the washing machine and air dried.

89.

REUSABLE KITCHEN TOWEL ROLL

A spill on the kitchen platform? Bring out the paper towels. Baby's mouth needs wiping? Paper towels to the rescue. Need to wipe down a misty surface? Paper towels, where are you? Paper rolls in the kitchen are ubiquitous these days, but if you want to reduce, reuse, and recycle, how about piecing together a reusable kitchen towel roll?

What you need

Time > 1 hour

Makes 6-8

- ✓ An old thin towel
- ✓ 1-2 T-shirts or 1 cotton shirt/bedsheet
- ✓ Snap buttons
- ✓ Needle
- ✓ Sewing thread

How

- Cut the old towel and the T-shirt fabric/cotton bedsheet into 9-inch squares. Take a towel square and a fabric square, and place them wrong sides together.

- Stitch three sides of the assembled towel together. To strengthen the kitchen towel and ensure it does not 'bag' in the wash, sew two straight lines diagonally from corner to corner. Cut the corners if the inseam is longer than needed and turn the towel inside out.
- Iron the towel so that the edges are crisp. Sew the open edge together along with the rest of the edges with a thin top stitch.
- When you have 6 to 8 towels, attach the snap buttons – the yin to go with the yang – on separate towels. The towels can then be snapped together and rolled up on a paper towel stand. Use, abuse, wash – and repeat.

90.

ALL-PURPOSE WIPES

A spill here, a leak there. What would any home be without these? It's easy to keep your house all in order – without resorting to the ubiquitous paper towels.

What you need

- ✓ 1 cup white vinegar or rubbing (isopropyl) alcohol
- ✓ 1 tbsp dish soap
- ✓ 40-45 drops tea tree or lemon essential oil
- ✓ T-shirt/cloth, cut into large squares

Time < 30 minutes

Makes 7-8

How

- Mix all wet ingredients in a bowl. Fold or roll up the cloth squares and place in the bowl. Let them sit till they soak in all the solution.
- Squeeze excess liquid and store the cloth rolls in a glass jar. Use as needed and wash with your sheets in the washing machine. Make a fresh batch every month.

91.

REUSE CITRUS PEELS

Brightly coloured citrus fruits are a ray of sunshine, especially during the winters. Chock-a-block with nutrients, every part of these fruits – oranges, kinus, mausambis, grapefruit, limes, and lemons – offers benefits. Don't forget to save the peels and process them into kitchen ingredients, body scrubs, and more.

How

- **Candied lemon peel:** Good to eat on its own, and great when added to cakes and cookies. Cut halved lemons into thin slices and remove all fruit pulp. Bring the water and lemon peel to a boil and then drain the water. Repeat this process thrice. Drain and set peels aside. Combine 2 cups water with 2 cups sugar, and boil till the sugar dissolves. Stir in the peels, reduce heat to low, and simmer until the pith is translucent. Remove and refrigerate if you like them sticky, or let them dry. Experiment with other citrus peels.
- **Lemon-pepper seasoning:** Save lemon skins (after making nimbu pani and the like) and scrape the zest off. Add peppercorns, and a pinch of coriander and caraway seeds.

Blitz in the mixer. Spread on a baking sheet, bake on a low temperature setting till dry, and powder in the mixer. Store for up to 6 months

- **Sugar scrub:** Citrus peels work wonders on the skin, helping reduce acne, wrinkles and patchy skin. Dry the peels, run in the mixer, and mix in an equal quantity of granulated sugar. Add coconut oil – and you have an aromatic scrub.
- **Orange oil:** Collect a sizeable amount of pith. Let it dry naturally. Place in a glass jar and top with the cheapest vodka. Close the jar (make sure there's room at the top) and shake. Let it sit for 4-5 days; make sure you shake it well daily. Filter into a bowl. Cover with a tissue and let it sit for 24 hours, so that the alcohol evaporates. Strain and use the oil left behind.
- **Potpourri:** A stovetop potpourri – orange and lemon peels boiled in water with cinnamon, cloves, star anise, and other spices – will leave your home smelling oh-so-great. For the dry version, bake the orange peels and lemon halves in the oven till dry. Mix with cinnamon, nutmeg, cloves, dried flowers, leaves, and twigs. Et voila!
- **Orange peel cleaner:** Toss orange peels into a glass jar and cover with white vinegar. Set in a cool, dark place for two weeks. Strain the liquid, pour into a spray bottle, and use to clean surfaces, countertops, windows, and more.

92.

Reuse Fruit Peels

It's human nature to toss out the peel – banana, apple, mango, and more – after the delicious fruit has been consumed. But using the peels puts every part of the fruit to use, ensuring that you reduce fruit waste. Decorate your table with delicious sides as you feed your face – it's a win-win!

How

- **Apple peel jelly:** Boil the cores and peels of apples with water till mushy, and strain. Measure the liquid and add half cup sugar and 1 tablespoon lemon juice for every cup of 'apple' water. Bring to a boil over high heat and cook, stirring often, until the mixture reaches the gel point. Let cool and then store in a sterilized jar.
- **Apple peel toner:** The pectin in apple peels makes them excellent toning material. Boil discarded peels with water for about 15 minutes. Let it cool, refrigerate, and use as needed.
- **Fruit face pack:** Often, fruits such as strawberries need their skin shaved off. That peel can be blitzed with yoghurt and honey to create an anytime face pack. Gunky pieces of mango,

papaya, and banana can also be mixed with yoghurt, lemon, honey, etc., to create face packs.

- **Mango peel syrup:** Many mango skins have a tough texture and bitter taste, so boil them with sugar and water to make a thick syrup that you can use on pancakes, to flavour lemonade, and more. Add a dab of lemon juice to enhance the flavour.
- **Mulled wine:** A basic bottle of red wine, dried orange peels, cinnamon, whole cloves, star anise, and some sugar come together in a saucepan. Let simmer for 15 minutes to an hour, but don't let the mix bubble. Strain, garnish with fresh orange slices and a cinnamon stick, and serve warm.
- **Pickled watermelon rind:** Remove the tough green skin and dice the watermelon rind. Cover with water, add salt, and refrigerate overnight. Rinse and drain well. Heat water, sugar, vinegar, cinnamon sticks, cloves, and peppercorns. Add rinds when the mix boils, simmer till tender and store in clean jars.
- **Fruit pulp:** Juicing is great for your system, but all that pulp going into the trash can doesn't seem so good. What can you do? Depending on the kind of pulp, use in muffin/cake batter, blend into smoothies, or add to ice trays to create fruity cubes.

93.

REUSE VEGETABLE PEELS

Think again before you toss those peels into the bin. Be it potato, tomato or cucumber, peels often contain as many nutrients as the part of the vegetable that is eaten. Why not harness all that natural goodness to create more recipes or to tone the skin? Rethink your veggie prep, and you'll see how much can be done with the humble peel.

How

- **Potato peel chips:** Place peels on a baking tray; drizzle with oil; and sprinkle with salt, pepper and other spices (cayenne, chilli flakes, etc.). Mix well till all peels are seasoned, and place into a preheated oven until brown and crunchy (8-10 minutes). Try with sweet potato/apple peels for a sweetish taste.
- **Cucumber peel toner:** Mix pulverized cucumber peels with 3 to 4 tablespoons of fresh aloe vera gel and distilled water to get a moisturizing toner. You can mix with yoghurt and honey to create your own under-eye mask. Or else, add the peels to a water pitcher to get refreshing cucumber water!

- **Tomato skin powder:** When a recipe calls for blanching tomatoes, don't toss the skins. Dehydrate in the oven (if in a sizeable quantity) and turn them into powder that you can add to recipes. You can also add the skins to recipes such as dals, soups, and curries.
- **Onion and garlic skin stock:** No Indian meal is complete without onions and garlic, but not many know that the skins we toss are an excellent source of vitamins, antioxidants, and flavonoids. Boil with other veggie peels (or with meat bones) to make delicious homemade soup stock.
- **Vegetable peel dip:** Carrot, zucchini, and cucumber shavings can make for great dips. Blitz in the mixer and add to strained yoghurt to make a wholesome dip. Try variants using carrot, radish or cauliflower greens. Vegetable pulp can also help make broths and scrambled eggs healthier.

94.

MAIN COURSE FROM VEGGIE SCRAPS

Who would have thought that humble vegetable scraps could get a new lease on life as something that could uplift your meals? Reusing kitchen discards lets us cut down on food waste and enjoy them in new, unusual ways. And think of the expression on your guests' faces when you tell them that the greens that are usually discarded created that pesto or salad. Can't be missed!

How

- **Carrot greens pesto:** Give your pasta a makeover by replacing the basil in the pesto with carrot greens. Combined with pine nuts/walnuts, it gives a new flavour that's sure to grow on you.
- **Radish greens sabzi:** Don't make the mistake of discarding radish greens: they pack quite a punch. Mix them with crushed ginger and garlic, chopped onion, and a smattering of besan to create a winter veggie that's perfect to be scooped up with ghee-smeared rotis.

- **Cauliflower/broccoli greens in a salad:** There's a lot that you can do with the green leaves around the heads of cauliflower and broccoli. Wash well and use them to add more green power to salads, soups, dressings, dips, and smoothies.
- **Watermelon rind stir fry:** Remove the tough green outer covering and dice up the rind. Toss in a pan with oil, broccoli, and carrots, and add seasoning of your choice to create a delicious stir fry.
- **Vegetable peel ravioli filling:** Vegetable peels can be disguised as an extremely delectable ravioli filling. Blend carrot, bottle gourd, and zucchini peels in the mixer with cheese, add seasoning of your choice, and stuff into homemade ravioli squares. Delish!

95.

REGROW VEGGIES FROM KITCHEN SCRAPS

Binning kitchen scraps is a habit for most of us, but foraging in the trash can help reap a good harvest. Garbage gardening – or using kitchen scraps to regrow vegetables such as lettuce, carrot greens, and spring onions – is the easiest way to keep fresh greens at hand. The best part? It takes zero effort.

What you need **Time > 5 days**

✓ Kitchen scraps

✓ Glass jars

✓ Deep dishes

✓ Water

How

- **Leafy, salad veggies:** Top salad picks such as celery, lettuce, and bok choy are the easiest to regrow. Cut off the plant's base (about 1 inch) and place the cut side up in a shallow saucer with an inch of water. Change the water regularly. These scraps do really well on a sunny, indoor windowsill. You can transplant them from water into soil when they show new root-and-shoot growth.

- **Bulb-like veggies:** Vegetables with swollen roots, such as green onions and leeks, can easily be regrown. Cut off the end with the tiny roots so you have 1-inch scraps. Place them (root down) in water of 1-inch depth; only the roots should be submerged. Change the water regularly.
- **Root veggies:** Carrots, beets, and turnips are widely consumed, but the top portion – with the leaves – is often tossed. Upcycle these scraps to grow your own microgreens for salads. Cut off the top so that half inch of the vegetable remains attached. Place in shallow water, cut side down, and fresh greens will soon appear.

BONUS HACK

ROSE WATER

Rose water has been used for centuries, and you can make your own – and ensure that you don't let that wilting bouquet go waste.

What you need **Time** < **1 hour**

✓ Roses
✓ Pot (large)
✓ Strainer
✓ Distilled/filtered water

How

- Remove the petals from stems and run them under cold tap water to remove any dirt or residue.
- Add the petals to a large pot and top with just enough water to cover them. Adding extra water will give you diluted rose water.
- Place the pot on the stove and bring the water to a boil. Cover and reduce the heat. Simmer for 15-20 minutes. Turn the heat off, and let the water cool (with the lid on).
- Strain and store in a glass bottle for up to a week outside and a month in the fridge.

96.

HOME COMPOSTING

It may seem tough, but isn't really. The good part? Composting cuts down on the amount of garbage your home sends to a landfill. Experts say around 30 per cent of what we throw away are food scraps and yard waste. Breaking down this waste can create rich food for soil, which returns nutrients to the land and improves its quality. Composting can be a part of your life, whether you live in a tiny apartment or a huge bungalow.

What you need **Time** > 2 months

✓ A large bin/trash can
✓ Food scraps
✓ Brown waste

How

- Compostable items are commonly classified into 'green' and 'brown' categories. Green items are plant-based, wet materials – fruit and vegetable scraps, grass and plant trimmings, weeds, and waste food. Brown items include dry plant material, such as dried leaves, twigs, newspapers, papers, egg cartons and corrugated cardboard.

- The 'greens' add nitrogen, which is a crucial element for microbial growth, while the 'browns' are carbon-rich. The browns are important as they allow water and air to flow – basically to get aeration going so that the microorganisms can do their job. Layering the browns and greens (keep them an inch or two in height) is vital, as is maintaining the ratio of three to four parts of browns to one part greens.

- Meat and dairy, fats and oils, and glossy paper are no-no's when it comes to composting. Compostable bags and wipes are not suitable for home composting; they work in industrial facilities. Using the right materials is key to get earthy, rich compost.

- Begin your layers and keep adding to them day by day. To keep things moving, and allow those superhero microbes to do their job, it's critical to turn or rotate the pile with a long stick once a week. Letting air in will ensure that the pile is wet, but not soggy.

- How long before you churn out compost? In hot climate, like we see in India, two months could do the trick. However, it could sometimes take up to four months. If the can smells like a dumpster, it's not decomposing; it may be too wet or the ratio may be off. Finished compost smells woody and earthy, and is fluffy when poked with a stick.

97.

UPCYCLED CARDBOARD BOX

Online shopping translates into a growing pile of cardboard boxes at home. Why not upcycle a few of those cardboard boxes into smart storage? Put those toys, magazines, books, files, napkins, hand towels – anything really – out of sight!

What you need

Time < 1 hour

Makes 1

- ✓ 1 cardboard box
- ✓ Spray adhesive/PVA glue
- ✓ Cotton fabric
- ✓ Laces and buttons to decorate (optional)
- ✓ Hot glue gun (optional)
- ✓ Stick-on labels (optional)
- ✓ Rope/paper (optional)

How

- The fabric should be large enough to wrap around the outer edges of the box and fold into the inside. Lay it down on a clean surface, right side down, and place the cardboard box at the centre.

- Using a pair of sharp scissors, cut out the corners of the fabric. Leave about half-inch of extra fabric on either side of the flaps. These can be folded in to give it a better finish.
- Give the bottle of spray adhesive a shake and spray one side of box (or else coat one with a thin layer of PVA glue, such as Fevicol). Bring the fabric up, stick it on, and press on it to remove bubbles.
- Spread the glue on the inside of the box, fold the fabric into the box, and remove air bubbles. Repeat on all sides. Time is of the essence, so paste the cloth as soon as the glue is applied. Make sure you clip the extra fabric at the bottom corners to fit.
- Cut a piece of cardboard about half-inch smaller than the bottom of the box. Spray with glue, cover with fabric, and place it at the bottom of the box. Decorate with lace or buttons (using a hot glue gun) or with stick-on labels. Other options include covering the cardboard boxes with rope or paper.

98.

BIRD FEEDER FROM A PLASTIC BOTTLE

If you close your eyes, the sound of birds chirping can take you far away from your apartment. Make sure birdsong is your companion every morning by hanging a few easy-to-make bird feeders in the verandah, porch, or from the branches of trees outside. This method gives new life to soda bottles, which are mostly always cut up and used as pen holders or flower pots.

What you need **Time < 30 minutes**

✓ A plastic soda bottle
✓ Two big wooden spoons
✓ Wire
✓ Marker

How

- Use the marker to draw a small circle on one side of the bottle, about 5 inches from the bottom. Cut it out with a craft knife and fit in the end of the spoon snugly into the hole. Directly opposite this hole, cut a slightly larger hole that will hold the big end of the spoon.

- Duplicate this process approximately 2 inches from the bottom of the soda bottle, but on the opposite sides of the bottle. The two wooden spoons should be at a 90-degree angle to one another.
- Fill the bottle with birdseed. Use the wire to make a crude hanger: twist it around the neck of the bottle a couple of times and then shape it into a bell-shaped hanger that you can hang from a hook or branch.

99.

MULTIPURPOSE TIN CADDY

Buying organizers, but they're not helping you stay organized? Keep cutlery, stationery, and more in place by making a vintage-style caddy that repurposes all those used food tins lying around. Baked beans, anyone? You'll need six cans!

What you need **Time > 1 day**

- ✓ 6 tin cans
- ✓ Wooden block
- ✓ Handle
- ✓ Screws
- ✓ Screwdriver
- ✓ Paint
- ✓ Paint brush
- ✓ Embellishments (optional)

How

- Remove all the labels from the tins. The best way to do this is to soak them in water mixed with a few drops of dishwashing liquid overnight and scrub off the paper the next day. Let the tins dry and paint them in a colour you like – brush it on or use a spray can.

- Paint the wooden block – either the same colour as the tins or a contrasting one. Use a block that lets you juxtapose three tin cans on each side and leaves space for a handle on top. Let it dry overnight, and then line up the cans to mark where to insert the screws.
- Drill shallow holes on your earmarked points, on the block and the cans, and insert the screws. Tighten with the screwdriver. Fix the handle on top and use screws to hold it in place - to easily tote the caddy around. You can put in anything you like – stationery, craft supplies, makeup, silverware.
- There's a lot you can do to upgrade your cans than just painting. Try sticking on fabric scraps, glue on burlap panels/ chalk labels, give them a coat of chalk paint, or affix stickers/ buttons.

100.

HOST A SWAP PARTY

Gather your family and friends, and tell them to get all their excess stuff for this nifty, thrifty get-together. Good for you, good for your home, and good for the environment. Anywhere between five to twenty people will ensure a good variety of items and get everyone swapping.

What you need **Time = An afternoon/evening**

✓ Lots of pre-loved items
✓ Sticky notes
✓ Pens
✓ A terrace/living room
✓ Snacks

How

- Set the ground rules. It's imperative that all the goods are of the same quality, so no one feels short-changed. Ask friends to bring items such as books, décor pieces, apparel, kitchenware – basically, all that they used and no longer do. They should all be pre-loved and gently used. Ask your guests to get a tote bag to take home their finds.

- The items may be used, but displaying them in a chic manner will make your guests want to snap them up. Set up a few tables, offer hangers, and switch to mood lighting to set the mood. Sort the display into categories: clothing, books, crafts, toys, games, cups, candles, and more.
- You can draw straws or chits to figure out who shops first. Keeping the number of items to three per turn will keep things moving and ensure fair distribution. Hand out tokens to ensure a person goes back with the same number of items they brought in.
- A personal recommendation or memory from guests is sure to draw interest. Hand out sticky notes so that they can write a small memo for each item. There's sure to be someone who wants that book you never read or that book you thumbed through 10 times. Ask guests to bring in snacks and serve cocktails towards the end so everyone goes home happy.

NOT THE END

'What we call the beginning is often the end. And to make an end is to make a beginning. The end is where we start from.'

–TS Eliot

For the longest time, I believed the end was just that: *the end*.

The ending was the last part of something; the final part that unflinchingly followed the beginning; the conclusion that inevitably brought a sense of closure. Now, bazillions of full moons later, I know the end doesn't imply what we assumed happened when the closing credits of a movie ran.

The end is where things actually begin.

The last chapter of this book is not the end of my journey towards a self-sufficient lifestyle – nor should it be yours. Truth be told, there can be no end to the quest towards self-sufficiency. It's a journey that must continue, an odyssey that needs to endure. The pursuit of a self-sufficient lifestyle may not be easy, but it's possible to hack your way to self-subsistence. After all, the idea of simple, self-sufficient living isn't new.

Jesus is said to have lived the simplest kind of life, encouraging his disciples 'to take nothing for their journey except a staff – no bread, no bag, no money in their belts – but to wear sandals and not put on two tunics'. Throughout the history of humanity, many have lived this way – great leaders like Gautam Buddha, Francis of Assisi and Henry David Thoreau to name a few.

Closer home, Mahatma Gandhi sowed the seeds of the Make-in-India initiative decades ago to encourage self-reliance. The Father of the Nation suggested that people *can* and *should* be able to produce their own necessities, including clothing, food and dwelling. His decision to wear yarn that had been hand-spun on a charkha, was in part asceticism and in part a way to simplify his lifestyle in solidarity with India's poor.

Spinning our own cloth may seem a tad too much for most of us, spoilt by the vagaries of fast fashion, but perhaps it wouldn't be a bad idea to give slow, simple, and self-sufficient living a whirl. Especially at a time when the world has become a sing-song chorus of 'me, me, me', 'want, want, want', 'more, more, more'.

LESSONS FROM JAPAN

In a world seeking perfection it is important to remember, the Japanese philosophy of *Wabi Sabi*. It appreciates beauty that is 'imperfect, impermanent, and incomplete' and celebrates a lifestyle that's more connected – to the world around us and to our inner selves.

An extension of this is the *Kintsugi* technique, the almost 500-year-old Japanese art of putting together broken pottery pieces with lacquer mixed with gold dust. It's a lesson in accepting and celebrating cracks, scars, and flaws – and creating an even more powerful work of art. We live in a time of mass production, quick buying decisions, and quicker disposal, and learning to repair, mend, and make do is a powerful lesson in life and sustainability.

In *The Psychology of Money: Timeless Lessons on Wealth, Greed, and Happiness*, Morgan Housel touches upon Kurt Vonnegut's eponymous poem '*Joe Heller*', published in the *New Yorker*.

Describing a party that the author of *Catch-22* and Vonnegut attended at a billionaire's house, the poem focuses on a small incident that encompasses the learnings of a lifetime. Vonnegut asks Heller how he feels about the fact that their host, a hedge fund manager, had made more money in one day than Heller had earned from *Catch-22* over its whole history. Heller's riposte has the power to silence everyone, even today. His wealth, said Heller, is 'the knowledge that I've got ENOUGH'.

An important part of surviving the journey to being self-sufficient is knowing how much is enough – for you!

In a world besieged by materialism and greed, taking a step back to learn the ethics of self-sufficiency would stand everyone in good stead. And a course in *rasquachismo*, the art of 'making do' and 'making the most from the least', would help further.

THE RASQUACHE AESTHETIC

In Spanish, *rasquache* means 'leftover' or having 'no value'. It is loaded with negative connotation, and *rasquachismo* is often used to describe an attitude that is 'of lower class, in bad taste, or too frugal'. If we detach it from the connotations imposed on the word, *rasquache* – often associated with America's Mexican Chicanx communities – exemplifies the aesthetic of 'making do'.

Rasquachismo celebrates this and the art of how to 'make the most from the least'. It's now seen as the 'view of the underdog, which combines inventiveness with a survivalist attitude', and is often found in the use of throwaway items such as broken plates, heaps of plastic, recycled wire, and faded plastic flowers for decorating. The philosophy highlights creativity and uniqueness that's put to use to give new life (and function) to something conventionally considered broken or 'useless'. Much like the DIY aesthetic!

NOT THE END

The reasons for making this voluntary lifestyle choice and it cannot work unless it is voluntary – are many, but the main philosophy is one: to be a part of the solution, not the problem.

Our quest for constant upgrading and enhancement has brought us to a point where we think nothing of things we do every single day: buy, use, toss.

We are making more, spending more, owning more, and throwing more. The result? An extremely fast-paced life, an unappeasable desire to make more money, and a detrimental attachment to wealth and possessions. Yet, as the world becomes increasingly complex, chaotic and confusing, we find ourselves yearning for the days gone by. For a simpler, more meaningful life filled with joy, laughter, and love.

Becoming self-sufficient will not fix all our problems at once, but it can be a first step towards thoughtful consumption, constant recycling and reuse, wresting back control of your life and, most importantly, a sustainable future. The goal of sustainability may seem far-fetched in the beginning, but it is definitely attainable. It isn't a quick-fix process; it's a long and gradual one, one that needs to be worked at consistently and constantly. At the very least, this book will help make adulting a wee bit easier.

A simple self-sufficient life is about rejecting complications wherever possible. It's about making a conscious choice to not chase the new and be happy with the old, live with less for longer, and enjoy the small things – to lead a healthier, heartier, and happier life.

NOTES

Section 3: Beauty

1. 'Audrey Hepburn Named World's Most Beautiful Woman'. Yahoo News. January 2015, https://tinyurl.com/s9jvt54n
2. Ibid.
3. Nitesh Chouhan, Himanshu Vig and Roshan Deshmukh, 'Cosmetics Market by Category (Skin and Sun Care Products, Hair Care Products, Deodorants & Fragrances, and Makeup & Color Cosmetics), Gender (Men, Women, and Unisex), and Distribution Channel (Hypermarkets/Supermarkets, Specialty Stores, Pharmacies, Online Sales Channels, and Others): Global Opportunity Analysis and Industry Forecast, 2021–2027', Allied Market Research, February 2021, https://www.alliedmarketresearch.com/cosmetics-market.
4. Kim Bhasin. 'Estee Lauder Says 'Lipstick Index' Is Out, Moisturizer Is In'. August 2020. https://www.bloomberg.com/news/articles/2020-08-20/estee-lauder-says-lipstick-index-is-out-moisturizer-is-in#xj4y7vzkg

Section 4: Health and Well-being

1. 'India Ayurvedic Products Market: Industry Trends, Share, Size, Growth, Opportunity and Forecast 2022-2027'. iMarc. https://www.imarcgroup.com/india-ayurvedic-products-market
2. Rosabeth Moss Kanter, 'The First Secret of Success Is Showing Up', *Harvard Business Review*, 14 February 2013, https://hbr.org/2013/02/the-first-secret-of-success-is.html.

Section 5: Reuse and Recycle

1. Ian Tiseo, 'Waste management in India - statistics & facts', Statista.com, 4 February 2022, https://www.statista.com/topics/5586/waste-management-india/,
2. Taran Deol, 'PM calls for week-long garbage-free country, but India is the world's highest waste-generator', The Print, 11

August 2020, https://theprint.in/india/pm-calls-for-week-long-garbage-freecountry-but-india-is-the-worlds-highest-waste-generator/478889/.

3. Ibid.
4. 'A "natural" rise in sustainability around the world', Nielsen IQ, 10 January 2019, https://www.nielsen.com/eu/en/insights/article/2019/a-natural-rise-in-sustainability-around-the-world/.

ABOUT THE AUTHOR

Teja Lele changed twelve schools in as many years, and credits her adaptability to her army-brat upbringing. Inspired by *The Fountainhead*, she trained as an architect but soon realized her building blocks were words and sentences, not bricks and concrete. An editor for twenty years, she has been DIYing ever since she discovered the joy of making over and upcycling. She loves to read, watch crime on the telly, and believes the best stories are found between the pages of a passport.